SPEAK UP!

How to ask for what you want, talk about what matters and make yourself heard

Helen Ponting

R∃THINK PRESS

First published in Great Britain in 2019
by Rethink Press (www.rethinkpress.com)

Contents

Introduction

'Be brave enough to start a conversation that matters.'
  — **Margaret Wheatley**

While anyone, at any age or stage of their life, can find conversations challenging, I've found in my career as a police officer that it's frequently younger people who have the most difficulties. Whether you're starting out on further education or stepping onto a new career path, you may find yourself in new conversation situations that challenge you. If you struggle with saying 'no', standing up for yourself with friends or family, or making yourself heard by people in authority, you'll find help in this book. Perhaps those challenging conversations – the ones we all have, in which we doubt ourselves and our abilities – are taking place in your head? Don't worry – help is at hand.

Having spent the last twenty-six years as a police officer, I have had to hold conversations with people from all walks of life. I have had to interview witnesses and suspects, deliver good news and bad news, and deal with people who really did not want to talk to the police and those who had no one else to turn to.

I have learned to hold conversations with just about anyone: people whose first language is not English; people with learning difficulties or hearing or sight impairments; angry people and desperate people. In doing so I have found that, no matter who you are speaking to, finding common ground is the best way to get to know them or get them to interact with you. Once you can do this, you will be able to understand people, help them, or make new friends and acquaintances.

Conversations are part of everyday life: at work, with colleagues or customers, during those important interviews or job appraisals, and, just as importantly, with family and friends. So, let me ask you some questions:

- Do you have trouble starting conversations because you don't know what to say?

- Do you lack confidence and feel like you have nothing of importance to add?

- Do you miss out on learning more about people or letting people find out more about you?

- Are you asking the right questions but not getting the answers you expect?

- When you have had work appraisals or interviews, have you ever felt that you have not given yourself the best chance?

If the answer to some or all these questions is 'yes', the five-step SPEAK system that you will learn in this book can help you to change how you approach conversations. The book will examine why conversations fail, how you can plan your interactions with others more constructively, and how to give yourself the best chance to have a really good conversation.

Many of you will consider that a conversation is something that you have between your family and friends when discussing how the day has been, what you have been up to or the plans you have for the week ahead. But conversations can be so much more than just chatting or making small talk. A single conversation could be the start of your dreams, so it is important for you to get this right, to be confident in holding conversations of all shapes and sizes, and to give yourself the best start to the future that you really want.

Young people in particular have many choices to make as they approach their final years of secondary education with the prospect of choosing their future careers. What will you do? What do you want to do? Many of you will be influenced by your parents, family or peers, and, to a certain extent, by what you see on the many social media streams that are available to you.

But do you make a considered judgement on what you want to do? Are you asking the right questions before you take that next important step? Or are you afraid to ask, scared of failure, losing face, or just simply not knowing what to say? Are you perhaps too afraid to disagree with the people advising you? All too often I have come across young people who have 'dropped out' of further education because they are 'not enjoying it' or have 'made the wrong choice'; they then feel that they have wasted their time and everybody else's, and, in some cases, wasted money.

When you finally get an interview, you may panic, ramble on, or completely dry up, which makes you feel stupid, adding to the fear and anxiety the next time you go for an interview. The more this happens, the more down on yourself you get, and you start to feel useless or that you will never get through an interview, and so the cycle continues. The negative conversations in your head increase, reducing your ability to progress.

This book will equip you with the tools to hold conversations about your future, your fears, your plans and concerns that are stopping you achieving your full potential, with your family, friends, and peers, and give you the opportunity to choose the path that is right for you and for your skills and talents. It will also give you the knowledge to plan, prepare, and be confident in interviews, asking the right questions, listening to the interviewer, and using the experiences that you already have to influence the way a conversation may go.

It's not just a case of changing the way you think. I'll provide you with a set of tools that can be applied in many different scenarios and situations, using the knowledge and experiences that you already have to greater effect. You will have many experiences and sources of knowledge, but you probably just haven't realised it yet. Once you are comfortable with the steps in this book you will find that you will start to enjoy your conversations more, be yourself in them, and feel more confident.

This book is designed to be a toolkit to help you explore your own knowledge and conversation style, but at the same time giving you essential points to consider. The sections will take you through logical steps to understand how conversations and communications work, and to identify some of the barriers to a good conversation. We'll move through the five steps, explaining why each step is important but also providing you the opportunity to examine and develop your own understanding, strengths and weakness in conversations. You may find some of the sections challenging as you seek to improve your confidence by confronting your fears and testing new ideas. Finally, we'll look at some of the most challenging conversations you may ever need to have, how to create a safe space in which to have these conversations, and how you can get through them successfully.

PART ONE

WHY ARE CONVERSATIONS SO CHALLENGING?

CHAPTER 1

Why Conversations Are Important

'The most important thing to know about statistics is that you don't have to be a statistic.'
  — **Adam Kirk Smith**

Some people will be lucky and be able to chat with anyone, but for most people conversing with strangers can be quite a daunting and overwhelming thing to do. Like most people, I sometimes felt that I had nothing of value to add or that I was not as intelligent as the person I was trying to speak to. And why would they want to listen to me anyway?

This all changed when I joined the police service and learned about conversation and interviewing skills. Over the years I have perfected these skills, and I've gone on to teach others, including police officers and other police service staff, and help them develop. Now, as a retired police officer and trainer, I want to share some of these skills with you so that you can have meaningful conversations with just about anyone – and that includes at interviews or career appraisals.

So, what did learning these new skills change for me? For one thing, I realised that I have a story to tell and experiences to share that are different from others' and that they also have their own stories to share that will be interesting or motivating. All you need is to be able to ask the right questions, share experiences, and listen to what is being said or not said. It takes a bit of practice to master the skills, but it will click for you like it did for me, and you will soon be holding conversations with ease and confidence. The more time you spend developing your skills the better you will become and the easier your conversations will be.

There are many different types of conversation you'll encounter over your lifetime; from intimate sharing of secrets to important fact finding, all conversations are important in their own way. We're going to look at several of the most challenging and important conversation topics you might need to address. These will provide a framework for all conversations, and you can adapt them as needed.

Challenging types of conversations people have today are about:

- Bullying

- Sexuality

- Exploring career options

- Pregnancy

- Religion

- Mental health

  - Substance misuse

  - Suicide

- Body image concerns

These are all incredibly important conversations that may change the course of your life. When you are able to use the SPEAK method you'll have these conversations fluently, and you'll be able to help others too.

Living a happy life

Talking and chatting with others is a great way to relax, make new friends, and share life experiences. In general, people are social creatures and need inter-action to thrive and be happy, to love and be loved. Sharing your day and listening to others – the highs, lows, experiences, and funny occurrences – helps you and your friends reflect on the day, work through any concerns or problems that you face, and find solutions or answers.

Don't bottle things up or refuse to talk to others about them, otherwise issues will just build and build. Being dishonest with yourself or avoiding talking about your fears or unhappiness will only build and create other issues that will affect your mental well-being, leading to stress and depression. Share and let your emotions out to reduce the impact of worries and stresses on your health, allowing you to live the life that you deserve and strive to have.

The world is full of many cultures, beliefs, and religions; faith is an important part of our lives but talking about it can be difficult as faith is a very personal thing about which people are often sensitive. Be considerate and respectful – as you might otherwise offend someone – and remember that some people do not have any faith, religion, or belief system. You don't have to avoid talking about your religion, and you can mention things you do to celebrate it, but you must realise that not everyone worships the same way as you. We all have so much to learn from each other and discussing our religions and beliefs can lead to a better understanding of others and different cultures. However, during casual conversations at school, college or work never try to persuade anyone to convert to your faith.

Reaching out

Conversations are essential in making and developing new friendships and finding a life partner. At times you will be chatting about something of interest to you and find that it is a source of common ground for all involved, and this can help reduce your stress and anxieties. Remember that conversations are two-way, and all participants should respect each other, empathise with each other, and develop their knowledge of each other.

Of course, conversations aren't just for social events with family and friends; you may meet someone casually, for example on the bus or train, and start to talk. These conversations can lead to forming relationships that become an important part of your life and your future happiness. With a potential romantic partner, you will discuss how you want your relationship to develop and when is the right time to start an intimate relationship, and you will be able to say 'no' if you are not ready, in the knowledge and belief that your new boy/girlfriend is listening to you and your wishes. You will discuss the right time to start a family, how many children you will have, and where you will live; you need to have conversations about all these aspects of your life together for you to be happy and fulfilled.

Good conversation is an important part of all romantic relationships, but remember that all relationships will have ups and downs. Healthy conversations can make it easier for you to deal with conflict and to build a stronger and healthier relationship together. Talk to each other as, no matter how well you think that you know and love each other, you cannot read your partner's mind. You need to have conversations that clearly state how you are feeling to avoid misunderstandings that may cause hurt, anger, resentment, or confusion.

Continuing your education

If you are planning to continue your education, you may find that the following information will help you prepare your personal statement and for any interview you may have to undertake.

Over the last twelve years, the ACS International Schools have commissioned a survey among university admissions officers to identify the qualities that a student requires to succeed in higher education.[1] The 2017 survey from eighty-one admissions officers in the UK shows that 49% of sixth formers are not sufficiently prepared for a successful transition from school to university. The report adds that failure to transition well to university can be of crucial importance as feeling unsettled and sad in the first year of university can be a shattering experience. University admissions officers have identified qualities that

---

1   *University Admissions Officers Report 2017*, ACS International Schools

they will look for in an application from students, regardless of the course they have chosen to do.

The qualities are:

- **A positive attitude toward study:** Are you ready to work hard and are not just applying for a good social life? Will you be able to cope with the workloads of your course at a higher level of education? It is not just about your grades and any projects or study that you have undertaken to improve and expand your skills and knowledge. You should also demonstrate that you are able to plan and manage your time.

- **A passion for the chosen course subject:** Why have you chosen that course? You will need to evidence in your application the reason why the course that you have chosen to study is important to you, what is it about the study that motivates you to find out more and drives you to understand and research the subject in greater detail.

- **An ability to think and work independently:** When completing your application, you need to ensure that you highlight your ability to think and learn independently and you will need to show evidence of your social skills and common sense.

- **An ability to persevere and complete tasks:** You will need to show commitment and determination to complete the course that you have chosen since 91% of university admissions officers looked for evidence of these qualities in applications. Your personal statement can include evidence of this, for example, holding part-time jobs or even being a regular member of a sports team will demonstrate your commitment and responsibility to a task.

- **An inquiring mind:** University admissions officers will look for evidence that you have taken the initiative to read up on your subject outside of the classroom. You can add this to your personal statement as it will not only emphasise your curiosity about the subject but also demonstrate your passion for it and your ability to think and work independently.

- **Good written English:** Do not just submit your first attempt at an application! Make sure you check it thoroughly and check again to make sure everything is spelled correctly and grammatically correct. Does it make sense? Have you followed any guidelines that have been supplied? Ask as many people as you can to proofread it and check its content. Get your teachers or lecturers who have experience in helping with university applications to make sure that it makes sense.

- **An ability to work well in groups:** Many courses require group work, and universities will want to see evidence of how you can contribute to the student experience; for example, being a part of the students' union, joining a society, or starting up a new club. Include evidence of memberships of sports teams or clubs or working with others in other group settings.

Finding fulfilling employment

Employers are looking for people with great communication skills.

The Labour Force Survey for the Office of National Statistics,[2] September to November 2017, for people aged from 16 to 24, shows there are:

- 3.86 million people in work (including 859,000 full-time students with part-time jobs)

- 538,000 unemployed people (including 182,000 full-time students looking for part-time work)

- 2.67 million economically inactive people, most of whom (2.04 million) were full-time students

However, the unemployment rate for those aged from 16 to 24 has been consistently higher than that for older age groups. It's challenging finding your first job. Learning how to have a great conversation during the interview will help you.

---

2   *Labour Force Survey* – Office for National Statistics

Looking at the figures from the same report, there were 810,000 jobs available between October and December 2017, and for the same period there were 538,000 unemployed young people; 182,000 of these were full-time students looking for part-time work. So, taken at face value and not taking into account any other factors such as role requirements, there was a potential vacancy for every young person. Just to put things into perspective, though, there were 1.44 million unemployed people aged 16–65 between September and November 2017, so there were not quite enough jobs for every unemployed person within that age range. You need to be able to communicate your value to any potential employer to convince them that you are the person that they need on their team.

What do employers want? What are your future employers seeking from you right now? Kent University, in consultation with a number of companies and institutions, has produced a table of qualities required, which I have shown below.[3] There is no ranked list of employability skills that employers will insist on and what they look for is subject to change, so always check with your prospective employer. As you can see, communication is on every list of skills that employers are looking for, which is the best reason to improve your conversation skills if you are looking to start a new career.

---

3 'Employability Skills', Career and Employability Service, University of Kent

What employers want

Prospects.ac.uk

Teamwork

Problem-solving

Communication

Time management

IT skills

Numeracy

Customer awareness

Jobs.ac.uk

Communication

Teamwork

Initiative

Project management

Flexibility

Interpersonal

Organisation

Warwick University

Communication

Teamwork

Leadership

Negotiation

Initiative

Time management

Organisation

Problem-solving

Customer skills

Commercial awareness

TargetJobs.co.uk

Commercial awareness

Communication

Teamwork

Negotiation and persuasion

Problem-solving

Leadership

Organisation

Perseverance and motivation

Ability to work under pressure

Confidence

Employers are also looking to recruit young people with a broad range of experience and the ability to demonstrate the wide variety of skills that they have developed through academic study, work experience, and extracurricular activities. While there is no definitive list of skills that every employer will want you to possess, the main skills that you should try to develop are:

- Numeracy/IT skills

- Communication skills

- Team-working skills

- Research/critical thinking skills

- Creativity/problem-solving skills

- Organisational skills

- Commercial awareness

It may be that you have already learned some of these skills over time. They can be gained from previous jobs, charity or voluntary work, your hobbies, or even just at home. These sorts of skills are known as 'transferable skills' and are a core set of skills and abilities that can be applied to a wide range of different roles and industries. Later in the book I will be getting you to identify your transferable skills.

Summary

The facts and figures show how younger people are represented in the employment stakes. The figures indicate that depending on the employment you are seeking and the criteria the employer is looking for there may not be a vacancy that is for you.

You need to make yourself stand out from the crowd for future employers and, as the above research shows, communication skills are highly sought-after by employers, and one of the reasons I have written this book.

Next let's look at what exactly a conversation is, and how you can communicate better and make yourself heard.

CHAPTER 2

What Is A Conversation?

'Conversation should be pleasant without scurrility, witty without affectation, free without indecency, learned without conceitedness, novel without falsehood.'
— **William Shakespeare**

Understanding the definition of 'conversation' will make it easier for you to know what you want to achieve or what you want to share during one. Conversations can fail, not just because of the people involved but also due to all the other things that can get in the way, especially in today's hectic world. Understanding why conversations fail can help avoid this happening to you. If you follow the guidelines below, your conversations will be much more satisfying and enlightening.

Conversation management

As a police officer you are always talking to people; colleagues, witnesses, members of the public, and of course suspects – quite often these are in an interview situation. The difference between an interview and a conversation is… not a lot! Interviews are more than likely to be recorded in some format – audio, video, or a written record – whereas a conversation probably is not. But the truth is they are both trying to find out more about something by asking questions and seeking answers and information.

Dr Eric Shepherd devised his Conversation Management model in 1983, to change the way that the police conducted investigative interviewing. He designed it so that the conversations would aid spontaneous disclosure from suspects, victims, and witnesses.[4] The Conversation Management model has stood the test of time and is now a proven, effective approach to getting evidentially sound results in many other organisations, not just the police service.

Conversation management not only forms the basis of my wide experience and knowledge and training in conversation and interviewing skills; it also has central values that will help you to understand the importance of managing a conversation.

---

4   Shepherd, E (2007). *Investigative Interviewing: The Conversation Management Approach*, Oxford, Oxford University Press.

Those values are:

- Awareness of how a conversation works

- Respecting and treating the person that you are speaking to as a conversation contributor rather than just bombarding them with questions or your own views

I want you to think about what you understand by the term 'conversation'; for example:

- How many people does it involve?

- What is it for?

- What does it include?

This is a good starting point to help you understand that a conversation is *not* just about talking to others.

While there are many definitions, the one in the online Cambridge dictionary is one of the best that I have found to reflect the extent of a conversation:

> 'Conversation: (a) talk between two or more people in which thoughts, feelings, and ideas are expressed, questions are asked and answered, or news and information is exchanged.'

This definition includes many of the elements that we overlook or do not include in our everyday

conversations and for that reason it is a good definition to remember.

Knowing the definition is all well and good, but to
have a successful conversation we must have some
idea of what we want to find out or what we want to
share. Most of us do not get the most from our conversations and miss out on nuggets of information
simply because we do not understand what a constitutes a conversation.

Why do we need conversation?

Conversations are not just about talking to or talking
at another person. As you have seen from the
definition above, conversations are much more
involved and are used to seek and share information,
thoughts, feelings, and ideas. So why is this important to us? Human beings live predominantly in
socially-focused communities, and, in general, we
need social contact to thrive. Conversations allow us
to socialise, and this in turn allows us to build better
relationships by understanding in more depth the
other people in those relationships. We can have rela-
tionship-strengthening conversations by asking the
right questions, empathising, and by sharing our
own feelings, aspirations, and inner thoughts. This
allows us also to be better understood and to develop
our self-confidence with others, and it also helps us
to take better care of ourselves and others. Without

conversations that involve sharing and balance, the chances are that we would become lonely and misunderstood, and could even be cast out from society.

COMMUNICATION TASK: HOW DO YOU FEEL WHEN CONVERSATIONS DON'T GO WELL?

Think of a time when conversations have not gone well for you. How did it make you feel? How difficult was it for you to start a conversation again with this person or even to start a conversation with anyone because of the fear of it not working out again?

Next time you have a conversation, think about the reasons why you are having that conversation and consider how you are feeling. Do you feel excited, sad, bored, angry, or happy? Think about why this is and whether you could improve the quality of the conversation and the way you are feeling. As you go through the book you will learn how you can do this so that your conversations can be the best they can be in whatever situation you find yourself in.

Communication facts

I will revisit many of these facts as we progress through the book, but I feel this is a good place to introduce them so that you are aware of them as you go. Based on the research, we spend on average 70% of our day in some form of communication.[5] The time

---

5   Adler, R, Rosenfeld, L, and Proctor, R (2001). *Interplay: The Process of Interpersonal Communicating*, 8th edn, Fort Worth, Texas, Harcourt.

we spend communicating consists of listening for 45% of the time, speaking for 30%, reading for 16%, and writing for 9%.

The average person talks at a rate of about 125–175 words per minute, while we can listen at a rate of up to 450 words per minute.[6] However, speech rate will depend on the language being used; for example, Japanese has the fastest speech rate, followed by Spanish, French, Italian, English, and German.[7] We only use about 25% of our mental capacity when we listen,[8] so 75% of our brains must be distracted, preoccupied, or forgetful when listening!

How do conversations work?

In an ideal world, conversations would be straightforward. We would just send our message in a language and terms (encode) that the receiver would understand immediately (decode), and they would reply with an answer or feedback that you would also understand straight away, as in the following diagram. Great, that's what already happens, right?

---

6   Carver, RP, Johnson, RL, and Friedman HL (1971). 'Factor Analysis of the Ability to Comprehend Time-compressed Speech', *Journal of Reading Behavior*, 4 / 1, 40–49.
7   Pellegrino, F, Coupe, C and Marsico, E (2011). 'Across-language Perspective on Speech Information Rate', *Language*, 87 / 3, 539–558.
8   Huseman, RC, Galvin, M and Prescott, D (1988). *Business Communication: Strategies and Skills*, Chicago, Holt, Rinehart & Winston.

Communication in an ideal world

As many of you have probably already experienced, it is not always as straightforward as that, and at times it feels like a game of charades. I remember a time when I was investigating a theft of a lady's purse from her handbag while she was shopping in a city centre where I used to work. The lady had unfortunately not closed her handbag, leaving her purse in full view of anyone who had the desire to steal it. The lady had gone back to the shop where she had last used her purse and spoke to the shop staff to see if it had been handed in. The shop staff had not found it but checked their CCTV to see if they could identify anyone who may have taken the purse.

A young male wearing blue jeans and a blue T-shirt was identified; as the city centre had a radio link between the shops the description of the young man was passed on to each shop by the next shop in the

29

link. A young man was spotted in another store and duly detained by the security staff as he matched the description they had received from the previous shop. The police were called, and I went into the store where the young man had been detained. In order to make sure that any action I took was lawful, I asked for the reason and circumstances of the young man's detention.

It was explained to me that a call had come over the radio link with a description of the young man who had stolen a lady's handbag in another store and that the lady had been left crying and upset. The security officer told me that this person matched the description of the offender given over the radio link. Although the detention was made in the belief that the young man was responsible for the theft, the description had been distorted as it had been passed between each store in turn. I did have a young man in front of me, but he was wearing black jeans and a blue shirt.

This story just goes to show how easily information (the message) can become distorted when delivered to another (the receiver), even when the information is clear to the messenger. With today's age of information and technology, and the multitude of channels that we can use to communicate, sending and receiving the right message is even more complex than it has ever been before – see the diagram below.

Multi-channel communications

> **COMMUNICATION TASK: HOW MANY WAYS ARE THERE TO COMMUNICATE?**
>
> A quick task for you: How many ways can you think of to communicate with others? Make a list and see how many you can think of.

I am sure that you have come up with quite a few: Facebook, Twitter, Snapchat, Instagram, face-to-face, mobile, telephone, text, etc. In 2011, there were roughly 5,406 ways to contact another human being![9] With so many ways to communicate with each other and with many having their own unique way to write

---

9   Stacy, S (2011). *The Way We Communicate: Pros and Cons,* The Next Great Generation. Available at: www.thenextgreatgeneration.com/ 2011/10/the-way-we-communicate-pros-and-cons.

or post, it is easy to understand how messages can be misunderstood, leading to barriers in effective communication. Today, there are probably a whole lot more, and this will only keep increasing with technology advancements.

Your message can be distorted by the channel that you select; for example, Twitter only allows 280 characters per tweet, so abbreviations are used, which can be misunderstood or not understood at all. Predictive text is also a great way to get misunderstood. If you do not check your message before you send it, you could have some fun replies or some quite angry ones!

I have a builder who does maintenance work on my house, and I have had some problems recently with some damp in the ground floor walls. The house is quite old, and the soil is up against one of the downstairs walls, so some work was needed to waterproof the outside walls to stop the damp getting in. The conversation in text with the builder went like this:

> Me: 'If you can do the work this week that would be great. Please can you confirm the price and which day you can start?'

> Builder: 'Dig trench to coach the tank and your boobs, DPN membrane, refill materials and labour £1,300. All work guaranteed.'

After much laughter and good humour, the work was completed on the walls and not on the tank or my boobs. But the mis-wording of the text could have led to a very different result, depending on who it was sent to. So *always* check your texts or messages before you send them.

As well as the channel you select for your message, noise is another factor that can distort your message and contribute to it being misunderstood – see the diagram below. With the added consideration of 'noise' and the everyday distractions all around you or the recipient of your message, it is easy to understand why conversations can fail.

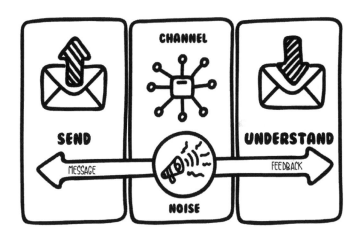

Distorted communications

COMMUNICATION TASK: NOISE ON THE LINE

Think about the last time you tried to speak to someone or call someone on your mobile when you were in a club, at a sporting event, or just walking down the street. What was happening around you that made it difficult for the person to hear you or for you to hear them? How many times did you have to repeat yourself or to ask them to say something again? This could be everyday things like traffic noise, sirens, roadworks, music, or other people talking; they are all sources of noise that can prevent your message being delivered correctly or you correctly receiving the message that was intended for you.

Life today can be so full and hectic that we sometimes do not hear the true message that is being sent and either second-guess or just hear want we want to hear. We then reply with a message that we think is the right answer, or provide feedback that we assume is correct or that will not offend. This can lead to further misunderstanding, annoyance, or impatience because the sender feels that you haven't been listening or are just being awkward, or that they have not explained themselves clearly enough. We then end up going around and around in circles getting nowhere fast.

How can you improve your conversation skills?

Now that you understand what a conversation is and why conversations can fail, how can you improve your conversation skills? This will not be accomplished by instantly learning a few skills; you will need to practise the skills that you are developing. Do not rush in straight away with the conversation that is the most important to you or your future. Start with a few straightforward conversations with friends and family; you may not think it now, but even these will need to have some structure. Remember the definition of a conversation; what are you sharing or trying to find out?

In the next few sections of this book, you will be learning a simple but effective way to master your conversation skills and manage the conversations that you start or find yourself in, sharing your thoughts and ideas, and finding out more about the people you are conversing with.

Summary

The definition of 'conversation' that I have chosen (there are many others) reflects the full scope of a conversation, not just 'talking at' or 'talking to' another. My definition requires thoughts, feelings and ideas to be shared, and questions to be asked and answered, in what should be a two-way process. My definition also highlights why, as human beings, we need conversation to understand one another better, to grow in confidence, to form better relationships and, most of all, to care for ourselves and those around us.

Conversations help us to explore the world and the people around us, to share experiences and seek new challenges, but they can easily be misleading or unfulfilling if we do not understand what we are trying to achieve with them, or if we are not aware of the outside influences that can change the message we are trying to send – to the point that it is completely different from what we intended, or has been embellished, or has relevant content missing!

PART TWO

HOW YOU CAN HAVE EASY CONVERSATIONS

Introduction: The SPEAK Model

'Seek first to understand, then to be understood.'
— **Stephen Covey**

In this section I'm going to introduce you to a brilliant model that helps you understand the importance of your communication. This model is easy to remember, and it's easy to break down the elements to plan and build your conversation structure. SPEAK is a simple five-step process that will help avoid failed conversations and misunderstandings, and help conquer the fear of conversations:

Situation – Consider the type of conversation you will have and how it is going to take place

Plan and Prepare – No matter what the purpose of the conversation, you will need to do your homework

Eyes and Ears – These are your most valuable assets in any conversation; use them to their full potential before opening your mouth

Ask Questions – Are you asking the right ones to get the most out of your conversation? Use open and closed questions at the right times

Knowledge – Use your life experiences and skills to support your conversations; you have a lot more knowledge than you believe you have

Where did the idea of this model come from?

Conversation management was introduced to the police service to enable spontaneous disclosures from witnesses and suspects by respecting and treating each person as a conversation contributor. My knowledge and experience of using this method and delivering training to police officers and staff form the basis of my rationale for creating the SPEAK model.

By introducing SPEAK I hope to bring a structure to your conversations so that you can get the most from them. You will need to practise, but a few simple skills will bring you confidence in conversing with others. Let's take a look at each of the steps in more detail so you can feel confident in conversational situations, including interviews and job appraisals.

CHAPTER 3

Situation

'The way we communicate with others and with ourselves ultimately determines the quality of our lives.'
   — **Anthony Robbins**

Remember I said there were many ways to communicate with others (5,406). Each one will have its own unique medium for conversation: words, pictures, emojis – you name it. So, being aware of which method you are going to use will give you a head start on a successful conversation. This is because if you know how you are going to communicate you can make sure that you are ready: Is my phone charged? Do I have enough minutes or data? Is the signal good? Is the location quiet so that we can both hear each other? Is the video link working? There are a multitude of things to consider even before you start the conversation.

Throughout this section I will be focusing on the conversation method, or, in other words, the way in which the conversation is going to take place; for example, will it be face-to-face, an interview, or over a telephone, including a mobile phone or video link? You will explore the different ways of holding a conversation, visit the current trends in communication, and identify some of the pluses and minuses for certain communication methods.

Finally, at the end of this section I will give you a short quiz to find out what sort of communicator you are at the moment. It's important for you to identify this at an early stage, so that you can adapt any of the future steps or practise different skills to develop or modify your present conversational style. As you will learn, not all conversational styles suit every situation, so you may have to revise your current style to be effective and to get the most from conversations.

COMMUNICATION TASK: HOLDING A CONVERSATION

Here is a link to my task sheet to make this easier: https://www.speakwithinfluence.co.uk/learning-support/; you can always continue on another sheet of paper if you run out of space.

In the first column, list all the scenarios in which you may have to hold a conversation (an interview, out with friends or

---

family, etc). In the second column, I want you to score how confident you feel about holding a conversation in these situations; use the smiley faces or number your confidence levels from 1 (not confident at all) to 5 (very confident).

Next, in column three, list the means of communication (face-to-face, mobile, etc). This list does not have to match up with Column 1; it is a separate list. Again, in the fourth column score how confident you are using each of your listed communication methods, thinking as well about which methods you use most or least.

Once the above steps have been completed, order Column 1 and Column 3 according to your favourite situations and the communication methods that you feel most comfortable with. Think about why this is – is it because these are the ones that you are most familiar with or use all the time, or is it for another reason? Remember your reasoning as you go through the rest of the section.

Now look at the bottom three of your ordered lists. Why are they there? What is it about these scenarios and communication methods that you struggle with or dislike? Now that you have identified these as an area of challenge you will be able to work on them as you go through the book so that you become more confident with them in the future.

Why have I given you this exercise? Hopefully by completing it you now have an idea of where your confidence and challenges lie and where you will need to do work depending on the conversation that you are holding and the method you are using.

The way we communicate

To put things in perspective, in 2018 the Office of Communications released figures about communication trends and the ever-changing landscape of communication methods in the UK.[10] These trends include the increase in the use of social networking sites to keep in touch.

Ofcom's data is grouped into different age ranges; where it specifies 'overall percentage of adults', Ofcom is referring to those aged 16 and above. I will show the age range 16–24 together with the overall figure as this is my target audience, although Ofcom also classes young adults as 18–34.

Ofcom's research revealed that internet use is becoming more mobile: more people are going online via their smartphones or other portable devices and accessing the internet in locations other than work and home.

- Nearly 88% of UK adults are online, increasing to 98% of 16–24-year-olds

- Adult internet users in the UK spend an average of 24 hours (1 day) per week online

- 16–24-year-old internet users have a higher weekly online use of 34.3 hours

---

10 https://www.ofcom.org.uk/research-and-data/
    multi-sector-research/cmr/cmr-2017

- While newer forms of social media are gaining popularity, Facebook is still the most popular, with 62% of adults having a profile/account

- WhatsApp usage has increased to 36% of adult users and is now seen as central to maintaining relationships with friends and family

- Four in five adults agree that new communication methods have made life easier, and three in five think that being online inspires them to try new things

- Two in five adults agree that they spend too much time online; this is more common among younger internet users (16–34) and less common among older internet users (55+)

- 77% of 16–34-year-olds agree that being online helps keep in touch with friends and family, but they also acknowledge that it interrupts face-to-face communications with others

- 78% of UK adults use a smartphone

- 95% of 16–24-year-olds use smartphones

- In 2017 the average mobile phone user spent 2 hours 49 minutes per day using their mobile phone

- In 2017 those aged 15–24 spent, on average, more than four hours a day using a mobile phone

- 57% of 16–24-year-old smartphone users would miss checking social media / messaging people if they did not have their phone

While the above research gives an insight into the current communication trend, what does it mean to us right now? Taken as a whole, the data shows that instant messaging has seen a significant rise in the last few years and is now an important part of the younger generation's lifestyle.

In general, the internet and social media are shown to impact face-to-face communication and are responsible in part for affecting our preferences at work or at home for communicating using electronic devices – even when in the same house or even the same room as the person we are conversing with.

Assessing communication methods

The table below lists a few of the best-known and most commonly-used ways to communicate with others. I have only included some of the pros and cons for each one and I hope that this will prompt to you think of many others.

Pros and cons of communication methods

Method	Pros	Cons
Face-to-face	• Held in real time • You can see and hear the other person and any body language or tone of voice • Can help establish trust and build a relationship	• You all must be present at the same time in the same place • Could prove expensive if everyone has to travel to the meeting/event
Phone call	• Held in real time • Distance is not a problem • Mostly instant access with no appointment • Urgent issues can be discussed immediately	• Need to focus on what is being said • Easy to accidentally interrupt • Quality of call can vary due to connection issues
Email	• Fast and free • Great if a face-to-face meeting cannot be arranged • Less interruption than with real-time communication as emailing time can be planned • Can share information and links with many others	• Replies are not always instant • Emails get lost in the inbox if it is not cleared regularly • Emails can carry viruses that will infect your computer

Instant messaging	• Held in real time • Free to use and quick to set up • Can share data, links, and photos • Live group calls	• Can get viruses from links and files • Can be time consuming as it's possible to lose track of time during a call or in sending or replying to messages
Blogging	• No spam • Can build an image as an expert • Appeal to large audience • Send messages in the format you wish	• You need to promote your blog, or you will not be heard • Not for personal messages to others
Discussion group	• Enables you to share your expertise • Useful for seeking community knowledge or help within the discussion group	• Can have restrictions about sharing • You might not get noticed
Wiki	• Useful for collaboration on projects • Content can have footnotes, links, and embedded files • Useful for seeking the Wiki community's help	• Time consuming to build • Skill needed to format • Slow interaction time

What type of communicator are you?

So far, we have looked at where you feel your strengths and challenges lie in conversations, what the current trends are, and some of the pluses and minuses of a few of the most frequently used communication methods. This is all relevant and great to know, especially about the areas you feel you need to improve; however, when you hold a conversation how do you get your message across? Do you shout people down, do you listen intently and then add your views, or do you rarely get to say what you want to say? How you converse is one of the most important areas to consider as this is key to the 'first impression' you make on another – and, of course, vice-versa.

COMMUNICATION TASK: WHAT IS YOUR CURRENT CONVERSATIONAL STYLE?

Conversations are part of everyday life, but how do you converse with others? On the 'Learning & Support' tab on my website www.speakwithinfluence.co.uk, you will find a short quiz to try; be honest with yourself and do not over-think your answers.

Once you have completed the quiz, the highest score represents what is currently your most dominant conversation style, although you may have a combination of them all.

Let us look at those styles and see what type of conversation you currently hold:

Column A – Passive or non-assertive
   conversationalist

Column B – Aggressive conversationalist

Column C – Assertive conversationalist

Column D – Passive-aggressive conversationalist

Conversation styles

As the quiz above shows, there are four communication or conversation styles. There has been much written about them in different books, journals, and reports, so I have just given you a flavour of the essentials for you to consider when thinking about how you speak to others.

When you speak, do you strongly express your feelings, opinions, and point of view, and do fail to consider anyone else's ideas and disregard the thoughts and beliefs of others? Do you swear a lot to get your point across? This is known as an aggressive conversation style and can lead you to becoming alienated, feared, and hated by others, seen as always blaming others for your failings or being immature.

With the passive-aggressive conversation style you will give the impression that you are smiling and cooperative and being helpful. But below the surface you will be muttering and doing all you can to undermine or disrupt the other person in a subtle underhand way. You feel unable to confront them and deal with your anger about them, even going as far as to deny that there is a problem. This can lead you to be alienated by others and fail to develop and mature, continually feeling you are powerless to change.

Passive communication is a style in which you will not be comfortable expressing your opinions or feelings to others – maybe going as far as to avoid standing up for your own values. You will remain passive even in the face of hurtful remarks, but deep down you will allow your grievances about these remarks to build up. Once you have reached your high tolerance level you will suddenly and without warning explode, letting all those repressed feelings out. But once this has happened, you will dive back into your shell feeling guilty, anxious, and confused because you feel that you do not have control of your life.

If you have an assertive conversation style you will clearly state your opinions and feelings and fight for your rights and needs clearly and appropriately, but you will at the same time consider and respect the rights and opinions of others. You will feel in control of your life, and you will be relaxed and a good listener and maintain eye contact with others while conversing. You will be able to rise to challenges as you are able to deal effectively with problems and issues as they arise, and you will inspire others because of the honesty and support that you give.

COMMUNICATION TASK: IS YOUR CURRENT CONVERSATIONAL STYLE SERVING YOU?

The above paragraphs are summaries of each of the styles, and you can find additional suggestions and facts about them by researching each of them online. You will find that depending on the search engine you are using and the site that you visit you will get different suggestions and examples of each of the styles. Do not take these as a definitive overview of each style; we are all different and will not display all the suggested traits. It is also important to remember that, depending on the situation that you find yourself in and the person you are talking to, your style may change to mirror that of the other person or to take charge of a situation or to follow another with more experience. Practise and observe others to see if you can identify the conversation styles and traits. Reflect on your own style and traits and see what works and does not work.

Keeping the conversation flowing

Conversations will not always be easy to keep going; there may be many reasons for this. For example, I had a student officer who found talking to the public a real challenge; they would avoid as much contact as they could and try to only attend calls that involved general policing such as area searches, parking infringements and the like. As you can imagine, this put the officer at a disadvantage straight away as most police work involves interacting with the public.

Student officers spend their first twelve weeks with an experienced police officer, and during this time reviews are conducted until the student officer is considered competent enough to go on solo patrol. The officer in question had been having difficulty throughout their tutorship, which had been extended. They would avoid having to speak to witnesses and suspects unless encouraged to by their tutor and, even then, they would take the easier route and ask few questions, and this was the same during interviews. The student insisted that they were fine and that they were just nervous and afraid that they would get things incorrect or say the wrong thing.

Once on solo patrol, with actions to help them improve their communication style and conversation with members of the public as well as with their colleagues, the officer still struggled. On one occasion, a police officer was despatched to speak to three young ladies who were having a good time but were being very loud and causing a nuisance. The officer allowed the girls to control the conversation and remained passive throughout, even when one of the girls started to swear and cause a disturbance. The disorder continued until another officer arrived to deal with the situation. This happened on several other occasions, and unfortunately the officer had to resign, not having the communication and conversation management skills to continue in the role.

The following example will show that you can improve how you communicate with others and achieve a positive result. A member of staff had to deal with members of the public at the enquiry desk of a local police station. This member of staff had face-to-face contact and telephone contact daily with members of the public and police officers. They struggled to be firm with people who were demanding and rude to them and to say 'no' to officers who were equally demanding when they wanted things done and did not consider the workload of the member of staff at the time. The problem became apparent when the member of staff started to suffer from stress and had to have some time off work. At a meeting with their manager, it was identified that the member of staff needed help to develop their confidence and assertiveness to overcome the stress that they were experiencing when dealing with impatient and angry people.

The member of staff attended a three-day workshop where they were able to identify their own communication style and were introduced to assertiveness communication. Once they understood assertiveness and its place in communications, they practised exercises to help build knowledge and confidence; this included working on body language and how this can set the scene even before they started to speak.

Over the course of the three days they practised different scenarios to help re-programme the way they had dealt with difficult people in the past and to become more positive and assertive.

The result was that the member of staff returned to work and was able to manage the difficult members of the public, still answering their questions and issues, but from a positive win–win perspective. They also became adept at saying 'no' if they were busy or not able to take on extra work.

Both examples show you that communication and conversation management skills do not always come easily and that you need to understand and recognise the different communication styles. It is necessary to practise dealing with them instead of walking away or avoiding the situation when it gets a bit tough; hang in there and share your experiences with others. You might have to be assertive at times, but it will be worth the practice.

Summary

This section was intended to get you to think about your own current conversation and communication styles. What are your strengths and what are your challenges? By doing the short exercises I hope that you have identified your strengths and the areas where you can practise conversation skills to gain confidence and to improve your skills. Practise in small steps, to develop both areas where possible; you could practise these with friends and family to experiment with what works best for you. We also looked at current trends in communication and noted that the internet and social media are affecting face-to-face communications – even when you are in the same room as the other person.

I hope that you took the conversation style quiz and have worked out what your current style is. Of course, this can change depending on the situation you find yourself in, but by understanding your current style and knowing about the other styles you can adapt your own style, or at least understand the style of the other person and manage the conversation using this knowledge.

In the next section I will focus on planning and preparation for your conversations. You have already started this journey by understanding your own strengths, challenges, and communication style.

CHAPTER 4

Plan and Prepare

'Let our advance worrying become advance thinking and planning.'
— **Winston Churchill**

Being prepared is essential if you want to get the most out of any conversation with others, and by this I do not mean being so structured that you sound like a robot or some sort of interrogation device. Careful planning and preparation will help calm your nerves and will make you feel secure and confident. Thorough planning lends credibility to your conversation and says to whoever is listening: 'This person knows why they are here and is ready to share their knowledge and skills.'

I will explain to you how to make sure that you have carefully thought about the conversation that you are going to have and the questions to ask yourself so that you fully understand what you will need for that conversation, especially if it is an interview. To help you achieve this thorough planning and preparation I will introduce two different methods: mind mapping and the use of sticky notes.

What is planning and preparing?

Planning may be defined as a thought process put into writing, analysing a problem and breaking it up into its component parts, then mastering each part and putting the parts back in the right order to make a logical sequence that is easy to remember.

Preparing is making yourself ready by practising skills and putting everything in the correct place so that you will know exactly where to find it when you need it, when that all-important question is asked.

COMMUNICATION TASK: QUESTIONS TO ASK YOURSELF

How many of you just hope that you will get the choices that you wish to study at college or university or get the first job that you interview for? Do you take the time to consider what you need to know about the course you want to study or the job that you are applying for?

Is it right for you? What skills do you have and need? When talking socially, have you considered your areas of knowledge and expertise that you can bring to a conversation, or the latest trends and news? These are just a few of the questions you should be asking yourself before you start any conversation.

Think back to the previous chapter and your conversational style; which style is your current one, and do conversations generally come easily to you? They can, with a little planning and preparation for those informal conversations that just start between friends or those you meet for the first time. Finding out about yourself and the people you are talking to takes practice and perseverance, so do not give up at the first hurdle if things do not work out for you straight away.

Formal conversations are probably more straightforward as you can plan and research prior to the event and be better prepared to answer and ask questions, but this will take time if you are to be ready for these all-important conversations.

COMMUNICATION TASK: GET PREPARED

There are several questions you will need to ask yourself at the start of the preparation and planning stage. Some of the most important ones are:

- Why I am having this conversation?
- Who I am going to have the conversation with?
- What is the conversation about or what do I want to achieve?
- When is the conversation going to take place?
- Where is the conversation going to be?
- How prepared do I have to be?
- How long do I have to prepare?

You will find a multitude of ways to answer these questions, and you may have used some of them when you have been revising for exams or course work, or preparing for discussions or interviews. For example, you may just list everything on a sheet of paper or may feel that you have everything in your head. But by planning and preparing you are giving yourself the best chance of remembering everything or creating a logical sequence to link your thoughts and make your conversation flow. Here are a couple of methods I use, and they work well for me; your results may vary, so experiment and see which method works best for you.

Mind mapping

Mind maps, which were created in the 1960s by Tony Buzan, are a simple visual way to organise your thoughts and ideas, and they are a great thinking tool to help structure and expand the information that you already have.[11] A mind map can then become a clear plan of detailed information which is logical and will help you remember the detail by using links. Unlike traditional note taking, mind maps can be pictures, words, or a combination of both; use what works for you when you are recalling information or expanding on the ideas that you already have.

Mind maps are easy to construct and logical to work your way through. You can use sheets of paper, white boards, or one of several apps available which are free or that you can purchase. If you are using paper, which I do find easier at times as you can use colours, pictures, and other representations to help your thinking process, these are the simple stages to follow:

- Place the thought or topic you are going to explore in the centre of a blank page in landscape format. You could use an image for your central theme, as an image is worth a thousand words and may help your thought processes. Starting

---

11   MIND MAPS is registered to the Buzan Organization under 'Organizing and conducting courses in personal and intellectual awareness and methods of self-improvement', all included in Class 41 **UK00001424476** (1993).

in the centre of the page gives you freedom to spread out in all directions and encourages you to be creative and express yourself more freely and naturally.

- From your central theme – the first level – add your thoughts and ideas to a second level surrounding it. You could put these ideas into different shapes so that you can distinguish between them. Join these ideas to the first level by using coloured lines or branches to show the link between them. You can then link the second level to the third and so on, as you expand thoughts, letting your imagination roam free, while you transfer your ideas to the page. Your mind works by association; the more it links things together, the happier it is. If you connect the branches, you will connect and remember your thoughts and ideas a lot more easily.

- Using colours and pictures throughout adds excitement to your expressions of creativity – colour adds extra vibrancy and life to your mind map and each image could represent a thousand words.

- You do not have to be a great artist as you can use photos or sketches from magazines and other sources; both will add energy to your thinking and it is fun to experiment with different colours and images for different themes.

- Use curved branches as straight lines are dull and will make you less likely to remember the detail. Curves tend to flow with your thoughts and ideas much better.

- Using one significant word per idea will give your mind map more impact and co-ordination, and it is easy to link single words between the levels and to remember the associations.

There are also apps for your digital devices that allow you to create mind maps. Below is an example of the free mind mapping app SimpleMind.eu (see below) that I used to plan the content for this chapter. As you can see, the app follows the principles of Tony Buzan's mind mapping, using a landscape profile, central theme with branches from it, and with each line featuring one key word. You can modify this model to add more key words and a few straight lines, as well as images and colour, to your mind map.

The great thing about apps on your digital devices is that the majority of the time you will have the device with you, so you can add to your mind map as things occur to you, whereas with the paper you will have to try and remember your additions until you get back to wherever the paper is.

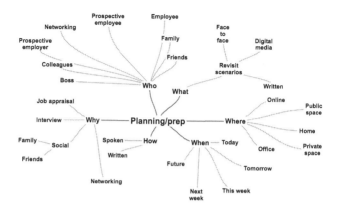

The SimpleMind planning app

COMMUNICATION TASK: MAKE A MIND MAP

Use the mind map template in the 'Learning & Support' tab on my website to revisit the strengths and challenges regarding effective communication skills which you identified earlier. Either do this on a big sheet of paper or download an app to your phone or computer for it.

Organising your thoughts

Another way of organising your thoughts and ideas to give structure to your planning and preparation is to use coloured index cards or sticky notes. The principle is much the same as the mind map method, starting with a central question, thought, or topic on a piece of coloured card or sticky note, then using a different coloured card or note to write down as many ideas or thoughts as you have to address the central topic. Then, for each of these ideas use a card or note of another colour to expand on it. Using the different colours helps to organise your thoughts and processes.

Whatever method you decide to use, you must refer to the job description if you are preparing for an interview or work appraisal. If you have a challenging conversation to prepare for – such as a challenging conversation about being bullied – put this at the centre in your mind map or sticky notes, then work outwards from there. If you are just thinking or planning for general conversations, then you can still follow this process but your notes will contain more personal detail about you and the areas you are willing to share. We will visit this again in Chapter 7, 'Knowledge'.

Once you have completed your planning and preparation you will need to keep revisiting your notes so that they become familiar to you and you feel more relaxed and natural when bringing them into a conversation. You may even find that as you review your planning you will remember other information or consider other questions that could be covered. Never just think that one look at your planning is enough; it takes practise to remember the detail so that you will do yourself justice in any conversation.

Planning in action

I have a couple of examples to share with you that demonstrate how vital planning and preparation can be and the consequences of not planning and preparing.

A friend's daughter applied for a position with a local company. The daughter had recently left technical college and was seeking full-time employment. She had been working at weekends in a retail store but wanted to find a permanent job. She had applied for a couple of part-time positions but without success. A particular vacancy became available, and it was her parents who encouraged her to apply. There were several other applicants for the role, so a face-to-face interview was arranged by the company to meet all the applicants. Since I was writing this book I offered to help her prepare for the interview. I asked her what preparation she had done; she had not done anything. I asked her what she knew about the company; she said she did not know anything. Finally, I asked her what the role was, and she was able to answer that it was office based and involved using a computer, but that was the extent of her knowledge of the work. I spoke to her parents to suggest that I might be able to help her prepare for the interview and give her some direction of what she needed to know. Her parents told me that they were going to go through the application and role profile with her a couple of days prior to the interview. Needless to say, as you have probably already worked out, their daughter did not get the job!

The second example relates to a conversation that I had to have with a principal of a technical college in the hope that we could work together to deliver a masterclass to sixth-form students about conversation management. While I was confident about the subject, I did not know about the role of the college, the current curriculum, and how my subject would fit in, and I also needed to find out a little more about the staff and especially the principal so that I would be able to engage with a topic or interest if necessary.

Out came my notebook and I wrote down all the things that I needed to find out. I could have done a mind map, but on this occasion, I decided on a simple list as I did not need to find out too much. The internet is a wonderful thing, and you can find out almost anything you want if you ask the search engine the right questions or put in specific search criteria. This was my first port of call as the technical college was not close to my home and therefore I could not just visit it to find out any information.

I found the correct site, the technical college's home page, and navigated around the site to find the answers to my questions. I found out about the role of the technical college, the ages of the students, and the curriculum that they were being taught. I also found information on the masterclass and previous speakers, and that my input would be for a maximum of 50 minutes. I found out some information about the staff and that the college had a Twitter account and LinkedIn profile. I also found that the college was supported by a well-known business and that students were encouraged to think outside of the box.

When I spoke to the principal I already knew a lot about the college and was comfortable speaking about conversation management and how it would develop and assist the students. The principal listened to what I had to say and invited me to contact the head of sixth form. The result is that I will now be running a masterclass on conversation management and interview skills with the sixth-form students.

Summary

This section concentrated on the important steps to take before you even start a conversation: finding out the context of the conversation. To be prepared for any conversation, you will have to do some planning. You will need to ask yourself the important questions about why you are having this conversation, what it is going to be about, when this conversation is going to take place and with whom.

To help you answer these questions and to identify other questions that arise, I have introduced you to a couple of ways to plan and structure your thoughts.

Mind mapping or using sticky notes are great ways to start with a central theme and then let your imagination do the work. Both are logical ways of linking pieces of information to one another, and you can use images, colour, and creative thinking to arrange your thoughts to help you remember the detail.

Of course, this is only one way of planning and preparing, and you may have other ways that you prefer to use. Experiment and see what works for you, but remember that whichever process you use should help you explore the question you are asking, help you seek solutions or ideas, and – most important of all – help you remember the steps so that you can link your thoughts and ideas when answering questions or discussing concepts in conversations.

In the next chapter I will explain to you the importance of your eyes and ears, and of body language, before you even begin to open your mouth to speak.

CHAPTER 5

Eyes and Ears

'We have two ears and one mouth so that we can listen twice as much as we speak.'
— **Epictetus**

We use our eyes as a part of communication as they reflect our sincerity, integrity, interest, and comfort when communicating with another person. Eye contact is a form of body language, and body language expresses more than words, so using your eyes to observe as well as to connect will speak volumes about you and how you communicate.

Our ears are not just for hearing; they are also for listening, and there is a big difference between the two. Hearing is receiving sound waves and vibrations from your surroundings, while listening is hearing a sound and understanding what you've heard.

Listening requires you to concentrate so that your brain seeks meaning from words and sentences, and this in turn leads to learning.

In this section I will explain that your eyes and ears are probably more important than your mouth during a conversation. You will learn that what people say may not always be what they mean. I will also give you some information about body language or non-verbal communications (NVCs). You may find that the people you speak with will tend to have much less conscious control over their NVCs than of what they are saying. NVCs are more expressive in nature than speech, and it is more difficult for a person to hide their NVCs as they are more instinctive. If there is a difference between what is being said and the NVC, you should probably trust the NVCs rather than the words being used.

Once you have learned about the importance of your eyes, ears, and NVCs, I will let you use your mouth, but even when using your mouth there are a number of things to consider.

How we take in the world around us

According to a document from Oklahoma State University, we use our senses in the following proportions:[12]

---

12 www.4h.okstate.edu/literature-links/lit-online/others

- Seeing – 83% of the time

- Hearing – 11% of the time

- Other senses – 6% of the time

Your eyes and ears are the two most important tools in your tool box. Your eyes will tell you much more about a person and their demeanour than your other senses will. This is then enhanced further by your ears: what is being said and how are they saying it, or are they just snarling and grunting at you? Your other senses also come into play – what you can smell, taste, and, in some cases, touch.

In my role as a police officer, I conducted many interviews with witnesses who were alleging that a crime had been committed against them. On one occasion I was called to the police station to speak to a woman who wished to report that her car had been stolen overnight from a city centre car park. The woman appeared quite nervous and would not make eye contact, fiddling with the rings on her fingers and almost whispering when explaining what had happened. You do expect some nerves because talking to the police at a police station can be quite daunting for some people, but as I asked more questions about the circumstances of the car's theft I could see and hear that she was not comfortable with what she was saying, and the story she was telling did not match her body language. She still would not make eye contact and would look at the floor or around the room but not at me. She had crossed her legs and turned to one side, almost forming a barrier to hide what her body language was saying.

When my questions probed a little too deeply into the theft of the car she would become defensive in her language and ask why I needed to know that, saying that she just wanted a report number for the insurance company. This, combined with the lack of detail in some of her answers, made me feel that the woman was not being completely honest about the theft of the car. I made a few enquiries with colleagues and the control room, and it transpired that the car had been found during the early hours of the morning in a ditch, and that enquiries were still ongoing with the owner. There was no damage to the car's ignition or any forced entry to the car. I challenged the woman with this information, and she started to cry and explained that she had leant the car to her son and that he had told her that the car had been stolen but later confessed that he had had an accident. As he was uninsured to drive the car, she had decided to report the car as stolen to get some insurance money to replace it.

COMMUNICATION TASK: WHAT IS BODY LANGUAGE SAYING?

Next time you are out, spend a little time watching other people's body language. If they are talking to others, do they appear comfortable?

By taking in both the body language and the words being said you can determine if you are being told the genuine facts. It is quite difficult for people to control their body language and takes a bit of practice. Utilising this knowledge helped me to realise that the woman's car theft story was not all that it seemed.

You need to develop your skills in using your eyes to read other people's body language and to be aware of your own so that your body and speech are portraying the same message. By understanding others' body language, you will be able to notice if they are telling you the same thing with their body as they are with their voice – a useful tool for managing conversations and adapting your style to suit them.

There are some NVCs that you will already be aware of, and you can always tell a lot by just watching mannerisms and facial expressions; we can usually recognise when people are friendly and approachable by their smile or willingness to speak to us. The same can be said for aggressive people; they will stare at you, puff up their body to make themselves look bigger, and, of course, combine this with an aggressive stance and clenched fists.

People who are not telling you the whole truth will generally avoid looking at you, their eyes and pupils will be wide, and they will fidget a lot. You need to be observant to what is happening around the person, as this may also affect their response to you. Is there someone else there with them who is influencing the response to you? Is this third party controlling the way a conversation is going? Does the person speaking to you have a sight or hearing impairment? Do they have any learning, psychological, or physiological disability that may affect how they respond to you? Also remember that some gestures and NVCs do not always mean the same thing in other countries, and they can lead to a different reaction than the one you expected.

COMMUNICATION TASK: RECOGNISABLE FACIAL EXPRESSIONS

In the circles below, draw as many facial expressions as you think you would be able to recognise. (Draw twelve blank circles on a piece of paper and fill them in if you do not want to mark your book.)

How many facial expressions can you come up with? Did you draw twelve, or was it more, or less? Researchers used to think that there were six expressions that everybody could identify: happiness, sadness, fear, anger, surprise, and disgust. A new study from the University of Glasgow suggests that some of those expressions share facial 'signals' and should be combined, and that there are now only four universally recognised facial expressions: happiness, sadness, fear/surprise, and anger/disgust.[13]

---

13 www.gla.ac.uk/news/archiveofnews/2014/february/ headline_306019_en.html

More about using your eyes

What else can your eyes tell you about a person apart from their gestures and mannerisms? The clothes people wear can be good indication of background and social standing, together with the sort of work or business attire their jobs require. But bear in mind that what someone chooses to wear is shaped by fashion, acceptable forms of dress, and even upbringing and age. We can all be influenced by our families, friends, and social environments at the time – the latest trend or fad. Be sure to check what constitutes acceptable clothing for a meeting, job interview, or social occasion; remember, 'You do not get a second chance to make a first impression'.

Eye contact is also a good sign that you are listening! Now, what have the eyes got to do with listening? Keeping eye contact tells the other person that you are engaged and paying attention to what they have to say. Use your eyes to build a connection with the other person; doing this could mean you like that person or you feel comfortable talking and communicating with them.

Be aware that avoiding eye contact could mean that you do not want the person you are speaking with to know too much about you, or that you do not particularly like them or are uncomfortable around them. This could lead the other person to read your lack of eye contact in an incorrectly negative way and produce an unsupportive feeling toward you.

Eye contact is vital to building trust with others, and a person will be more likely to trust and value what you have to say if you maintain regular eye contact as it shows an openness in your interaction. It also tells the other person that you are confident and self-assured.

COMMUNICATION TASK: PRACTISE EYE CONTACT

Practise using your eyes to improve your observation skills so that you notice mannerisms, physical disabilities, or other features that will give you an insight into how the person is feeling or reacting to your conversation – what they are expecting or are prepared for. Practise maintaining eye contact with the person you are talking

---

to; this will indicate interest and say to the person, 'You are interesting, and I am listening'.

Give this a go next time you are out: watch people's reactions to others and see if you can identify the different types of NVCs. Are they making eye contact with the other person? Get used to making eye contact with others; it could be when you are buying something in a store or supermarket or when speaking to friends and family.

Below I have included a table listing some of the NVCs that you may see and recognise when you are out and about. Remember that what you see may not always reflect what the body language means, so check what is going on around people and what words are being used in the conversation:

Non-verbal communications

Body language displayed	What it may mean
Standing with hands on hips	Readiness, aggression
Uncrossed legs while sitting	Openness
Crossed legs while sitting	Caution, disinterest
Spread legs while standing	Aggression, ready for action
Legs crossed while standing	Insecurity, submission, or engagement

Open legs while sitting	Arrogance, combative, or sexual posturing
Arms folded over chest	Defensiveness or disagreement with opinions of other people
Hands in pockets	Disinterest, boredom
Raised eyebrows	Frustration
Head nodding	Agreement
Head tilted to one side	Non-threatening, submissive, thoughtfulness
Head tilted downward	Criticism or reprimanded
Crossed arms and crossed legs	Probably defensive
Holding a drink in front of the body with both hands	Nervousness
Palm(s) up or open	Submissive, truthful, honest, appealing
Palm(s) down	Authority, strength, dominance
Finger pointing (at a person)	Aggression, threat, underlining a point
Clenched fist(s)	Resistance, aggression, determination
Steepled fingers	Thoughtfulness, principled
Touching nose, while speaking	Lying or embellishment

Your ears

The same recommendations for using your eyes can be made about using your ears to best effect. Using your ears is not just a case of hearing; it is about listening. Listening is a skill that lets the sound you hear go through your brain to process the meaning of the sound, and this requires you to concentrate on that sound or what is being said to truly understand it.

You can probably tell from the tone, level, or words that are being used by a person how they are feeling about their interaction with you or another person. What could they mean? Are they raising their voice or shouting? Are the words slurred and garbled? Are they quiet and not engaging? Are you listening to the words and the message that the person is communicating – even if this is silence? If we think back to the section on 'What is a conversation?', how much of their conversation is being distorted by the channel they are using? We must remember that accents, disabilities, terminology, and meanings – as well as the fact that the person may not have English as a first language – can all make a difference to the message or words that you hear and receive.

You need to listen carefully to understand the message that is being communicated. I have seen conversations misunderstood, and this leads to fights, neighbour and family disputes, arguments, misunderstandings, and complications, whether at home, school, or work, all of which could have been avoided if the participants listened to each other's points of view and did not jump straight to conclusions, or only considered their own needs.

There are five recognised ways to improve your listening skills and therefore help you to improve your conversations. They are:

1. Receive the message

Think back to the 'How do conversations work?' section. Receiving the message is the first stage of the listening process, and this is where you will need to take in the information being sent to you, whether verbally or non-verbally. Remember that not all communication is done through speech, and not all listening is done with your ears.

The key to receiving a message is to pay attention. Concentrate on what is being said using these simple guidelines:

a. Avoid distractions. This may be obvious, but do not have your mobile out, your headphones in, or the television on. Listening will not work if you try to divide your attention between the person who is talking to you and something else. You might think you're good at multi-tasking, but in reality you need to concentrate on listening and understanding what is being said; this in turn will make you a more respected person among your friends, family, and future employers.

b. Don't interrupt the speaker. You might want to guess what the speaker is saying, or what they're about to say, but do not. It's rude to interrupt, and you may find that you are completely wrong, which will not help your standing or cause, depending on who you are speaking to. To show that you are paying attention, though, you could practise your non-verbal feedback, such as nodding and smiling at the person who is speaking.

c. Don't practise your response. Only listen. If you start to plan your answer or response while the other person is speaking, you are going to miss things and may find yourself getting the 'wrong end of the stick' when it's your turn to talk. Remember: concentrate and do not try to multi-task as your conversation may suffer because of this.

2. **Understand the message**

Once you have received the information from a person in the conversation and have understood the message you can then plan your response. You can do this by asking questions or confirming parts of the person's message by retelling it. This allows you to demonstrate your active engagement with the person's communication and will help you better understand their message.

3. **Remember what the conversation is about**

This involves retaining the information in the message that has been sent to you. The best way to do this is to move the key elements of the message from your short-term memory into your long-term memory. Here are a couple of methods for doing this for you to try:

a. Recognise the essential ideas. Find the main points of the conversation to give you the key ideas in it; this will help you to establish an easy-to-grasp general idea of the conversation. Although the full facts will remain in your immediate memory, storing the main points in your long-term memory will help you understand the conversation better and remember the points for a longer time.

b. Make the message familiar. Relate the key points to something you already know. This should be easy to do – from your planning and preparation phase, the chances are that the conversation you are having will trigger your memories from your previous study and even your own past experiences. Use all of these to help you retain the essential facts of the conversation.

4. **Evaluate the message**

At this stage, you are still a listener, but you can start to think about your response. After completing the previous steps, you can now begin to sort the message into its component pieces; for example, you could ask yourself:

- What is fact, and what is opinion?

- What parts of the message, if any, were being embellished or exaggerated?

- What parts of the sender's message represent their own views?

- What was the purpose of the conversation (sharing, fact finding, etc)? Remember the definition of 'conversation'.

After deciding what the conversation was about, you are ready to reply.

5. **Respond to the message**

   Once you have received, understood, remembered, and evaluated the message, replying should be easier than ever. You will be prepared to continue the conversation and respond to the person's message and to bring in your own thoughts and understanding.

There is still a fine line between listening to the message and replying, and you will need to be aware that joining a conversation is still part of the listening process. Please consider these points before you jump in to a conversation:

Don't complete the speaker's sentences. This could be a disrespectful and rude way of joining a conversation to get your own view heard. It delays the receiving process and may cause the person you are conversing with to listen to you less or not listen at all.

Address the conversation points. If you have followed the steps above, you will understand what the conversation is about and will have prepared your own response. When you discuss the main points of the conversation it will be easier for the other person to shift into a listener role when they can follow exactly what part of their message you're referring to.

You are probably thinking that each step seems like a lengthy process. In reality, all of this happens in a short space of time, and by working on these steps you should start to feel the process becoming more natural and comfortable for you during a conversation. Practising will make you more aware of the way you communicate and more able to identify any bad habits you have developed that delay the listening process.

Listening is the most important part of a conversation because if you fail to understand the message being relayed to you then you will fail in providing a full and meaningful response. You must learn to take control of the listening process, and this will turn you into a better communicator.

First impressions

Did you know that that when you first meet a person, they will make a judgement about you in approximately seven seconds? Research results on first impressions vary, with some researchers believing it takes thirty seconds to form a first impression and others one to two seconds. A study by Princeton psychologists found it takes only a tenth of a second to form an impression of somebody with facial expressions alone.[14]

Whatever figure you choose to believe, it is true to say that first impressions are fast; you might not even have the time to speak before one is made!

The following pie chart will give you a great insight into what people focus on when meeting you for the first time or during a conversation. Research by Albert Mehrabian suggested that body language was the most important factor, followed by how you sound, with what is said being the least important consideration![15] There is doubt about the Mehrabian model as an all-encompassing theory, interesting though it is. Michael Parker has suggested an alternative formula:[16]

Words = good

Words + tone = better

Words + tone + body language = best

14   www.princeton.edu/news/2006/08/22/
     snap-judgments-decide-faces-character-psychologist-finds
15   Mehrabian, A (1981). *Silent Messages: Implicit Communication of Emotions and Attitudes*, Belmont, California, Wadsworth.
16   Parker, M (2014). *It's Not What You Say, It's The Way You Say It!*, London, Vermillion.

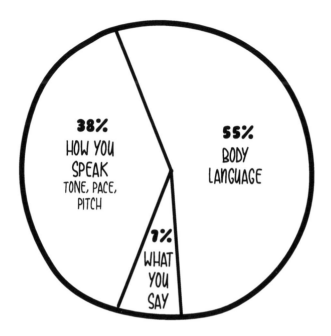

After starting the conversation with your eyes and ears, you can now use your mouth. But wait – what do Mehrabian and Parker think about this? Only 7% of our conversation interactions are about the words you use; while this is good to know it does not give you the full picture. The next 38% is about how you say the words, and this is better information because you can convey more meaning by using tone. Yes, the words that you use are important as they will demonstrate your level of understanding or knowledge, but it is how you say them that will engage with the person or people that you are speaking to. You could be sharing the most exciting thing that has ever happened, but if you say this with a monotone and bland voice it will not come across as exciting, just boring, and people will not listen or will take little interest in what you are saying.

The same can be said for the volume level of your voice when talking; if you are quiet or mumble, you will not be heard, and you may come across as not fully knowing what you are talking about or unconvinced or unsure of what you are saying. When you are nervous or excited you might talk quickly and in a high-pitched voice, which could sound like panic. If you shout or raise your voice you could be considered aggressive or arrogant; this may then put people off or make them avoid talking to you further.

COMMUNICATION TASK: HOW WELL ARE YOU COMMUNICATING?

Revisit the types of conversational styles and once again consider what your current style is. How is it working for you? Do people listen and interact with you or do you find that no one listens or that people talk over you?

Your voice can be as expressive as your gestures – smiles, frowns, movement, or body position – and you can express your passion and enthusiasm for a subject as well as your dislike or disapproval by changing your tone of voice. Be careful, though, that your body and gestures are saying the same thing as your voice; if not, this can lead to confusion and mistrust from the person that you are talking to.

The speed at which you talk is also important; if you talk quickly it can give away your confidence or nervousness to anyone that you are speaking to. On the other hand, of course, speak too slowly and others may think that you do not know what to say, and this could lead them to finish sentences for you or try to get you to speed up. Moderate the speed you speak at to show that you are thinking and deliberating on your answer before you say anything; this will ensure that your answer is considered and accurate without waffle or spluttering over words, and it will keep your audience engaged and attentive.

Do not interrupt or argue, as this is rude and could lead you to be removed from a conversation altogether. With practice and patience, you will find an opportunity to add your view during a conversation and to consider others' viewpoints; if we revisit the definition of 'conversation', this what it is all about.

When speaking you must ensure that you display calmness and confidence by using your voice to maximum effect; tone, pitch, speed, and content will all give you a great start to begin and continue a great conversation.

Silence is golden

While we are talking about using your mouth, silence is also a powerful tool in your armoury. It gives you time to think, especially if you have been asked a question that needs a careful response. It can also be used to prompt others to add more detail to something that they have already said. Human beings hate silences, and you will find that someone will always fill the silence with something, even if it is meaningless or random. So, if you ask someone a question, which they answer but which you feel they could elaborate on, just leave a moment of silence and you will probably find that they will continue talking...

Summary

This section concentrated on non-speech aspects that need to be considered when communicating with others. Your eyes will give you more information about the person and what is going on in their surroundings that may be affecting their interaction with you during a conversation. As you have seen, 82% of our impressions on the world around us involve our eyes, 55% of that being NVCs, gestures, and body movements. Taking note of what you see and understanding how this can help you to manage conversations will lead to more successful interactions with others. Understanding NVCs can be complex as there are so many different ones; it will take good observation skills and practice to make the most of your eyes. Always remember that many other factors will contribute to what you see and how people react to their surroundings or to you; learn and adapt to these factors to improve your understanding of conversation management.

Using your ears is as important as your eyes; if you do not hear what is being said, then how can you react or join in? Listen not only to the words that are being said but also to how they are being said, the tone that is being used, the pitch, and the pauses. Use your ears together with your eyes to take in the whole picture of the conversation, so that you can fully understand the motivation of the speaker and be able to respond accordingly.

When using your mouth, take time to consider how you are going to start your conversation and take your time responding. Speak in a calm and considered way, and do not raise your voice or argue; this will demonstrate to others your confidence and comfort when holding a conversation.

Putting your eyes and ears to work before your mouth will give you the best information about the person and the situation before you start or join the conversation. In the next section I will visit the complex issue of questions and how to ask them.

CHAPTER 6

Ask Questions

I keep six honest serving men
(They taught me all I knew);
Their names are What and Why and When
And How and Where and Who.
  — **Rudyard Kipling**

As human beings we start asking questions from an early age and continue to ask questions throughout our lives. We ask questions to seek information that helps us to plan things, to find solutions to our problems, or to find out about something that we do not know about. At times, we simply ask questions to start a conversation with someone or to make ourselves feel better. Understanding how to formulate questions can help you explore ideas, open up discussions, uncover truth, or simply discover more about a person you are speaking to. Questioning will lead to a process that will keep you learning throughout your life.

In the previous section we looked at the use of your eyes, ears, and mouth to find out about the person or people that you are communicating with. In this section we will look at how people can use questions to find out more about each other. I will be focusing on question types and the context of questioning, starting with open questions like who, what, and when, and then introducing closed questions and how these can be used effectively. Once you have grasped the use of the open and closed questions, I will then move into how you can use funnelling to obtain a specific answer. Lastly, I will touch on assumptive and problem-solving questions, which can take a bit of mastering.

There are two main types of questions you can use: open and closed. They are very different in character and their usage needs to be mastered to get the most from conversations.

Open and closed questions

The basic purpose of an open question is to receive a long answer. Although any question could receive a long answer, open questions deliberately seek a longer fuller answer from the person you are speaking to. Open questions are used to get the person you are speaking to think and reflect before they answer. They seek the other person's opinions and feelings and allow them to become engaged and involved in the flow of the conversation. I will look at how open questions can be constructed later in this section.

Closed questions can come in two formats: those answered with either 'yes' or 'no' (eg, 'Is this where you live?'), and those answered with a single word or a short phrase (eg, 'How old are you?').

As you may be able to see, the short-phrase closed questions can lead to confusion as they could fit into the definition for open questions, depending on the length of the short phrase. So, to keep it simple, you may find it easier just to think of these as open questions.

Closed questions give you facts; the questions are easy and quick for the person you are addressing to answer, and you can control where the conversation is going.

Closed questions are useful as an ice breaking question; for example, 'Isn't the weather great today?' This type of closed question can quite often start a conversation, and it can be followed by the open questions to seek more information about or from a person. Closed questions are also great for testing a person's understanding or clarification of a point, but be careful not to continually ask closed questions as this can set up a positive or negative frame of mind in the person that you are conversing with.

When opening conversations, which you will have now planned to get the most out of them, a good balance is around three closed questions to one open question. The closed questions start the conversation and can be used to review progress, while the open question gets the other person thinking and continuing to give you useful information about them or the topic you are seeking information about.

You will need to get them to ask you open questions as this will give you the opportunity to talk about the subject that you want to speak about. You could try to accomplish this by appealing to their curiosity with an unfinished story, for example. A word of warning, though: sharing too much information about yourself too soon can have the opposite effect. You can reveal too much about yourself, run out of things to say, or the other person may decide that they have nothing in common with you and clam up, or get bored and leave.

COMMUNICATION TASK: MAKE A LIST OF OPEN AND CLOSED QUESTIONS

Take a sheet of paper and make two columns – closed questions and open questions. Now list as many questions of each type as you can think of for the particular challenging conversation you need to have. Thinking about the types of questions and noting them will help you get prepared.

At the start of this section I included a short poem by Rudyard Kipling. He outlined a powerful set of questions, and these will be the basis for open questions that I want you to remember.

What?

Using 'What' at the start of a question seeks further information about something. 'What' can also be used as an exclamation of surprise (ie, 'What a great idea!').

'What' questions can include:

- What are you doing?

- What is your name?

- What books can I read on the subject?

- What is stopping you from succeeding?

Why?

Think of young children or people who are trying to find out the reason something happened. They will often start the question by asking 'Why?' If you know why people have done something, then you can gain a greater awareness of them. If you can work out how the world works, then you may be able to affect changes in your future career and life.

Using 'Why' can also be a good way of creating a pause or distraction in a conversation you are holding, as many people make self-confident statements but without knowing the real 'why' behind those claims. Asking 'Why' may help them to examine their thought basis and theories in more detail. Of course, you could always ask the question 'Why not?', which could prove an imaginative prompt for inspiring people to think 'outside the box'.

'Why' questions include:

- Why did you do that?

- Why did that happen?

- Why is it important for us to try it again?

- Why not give it a try?

When?

'When' is used to establish time, and can refer to two different types of time. It can ask for a specific time – for example, when a person will arrive or when an action will be completed – or it can seek a period of time, such as when a person will take a holiday.

'When' questions include:

- When will you be arriving?

- When will you be finished?

- When are you taking your holiday?
- When will you be making the decision?

How?

'How' seeks process verbs to identify a series of actions or steps taken to achieve a particular end; this question type can also be used to probe deeper to gain detail of what has happened or what will happen.

'How' questions include:

- How did you achieve that?
- How shall we get there?
- How will you know…?

'How' may also be used with other words to probe into time and quantity; for example:

- How often do you use social media?
- How much do you use social media?

Where?

'Where' is used as a question to find out the position, direction, or destination of something or someone.

'Where' questions include:

- Where will you put it?

- Where will it be delivered?

- Where are you going?

Who?

Asking 'Who' brings people into the conversation and links them with actions or discussions.

'Who' questions include:

- Who is going to the party?

- Who will bring the present?

- Who else would be interested?

TEDPIE

TEDPIE is a type of 'question' that is used in the police service during interviews. When used in the right context it is more of a command/instruction than a question, but it is one of the most effective techniques to find lots of information in one go:[17]

A question...

---

[17]   Fisher, RP, and Geiselman, RE (1992). *Memory-enhancing Techniques for Investigative Interviewing: The Cognitive Interview*, Springfield, Illinois, Charles C Thomas.

TED

Tell me…?
Explain to me…?
Describe to me…?

… combined with a probing word:

PIE

Precisely
In detail
Exactly

Together they will provide you with a lot of detail by asking just one question. For example:

- 'Tell me in detail what you think of the latest fad.'
- 'Explain to me precisely what you mean.'
- 'Describe to me exactly what happened.'

COMMUNICATION TASK: USING TEDPIE

Think of a challenging conversation you may have in the future. Using TEDPIE, write down an example for each of the TEDPIE words of how you can open the conversation. Don't forget that you can use any of the PIE probing words with any of the TED opening words.

Funnelling

You now have the basic knowledge of the type of questions you can ask to find out information, whether open, closed, or TEDPIE. All of these can be combined during a conversation to get the most detail or to explore further the answers you have been given; the latter technique is known as funnelling – see the illustration below.

In order to funnel, start with a TEDPIE exploration question to get a lot of detail. You will not be able to delve into all the detail given, so focus on something that you find interesting or would like to find out more about. Now you can use open questions to find out more about the point that you are interested in. Remember that this is two-way process and that you should not just bombard the other person with questions; if you do, they may just get fed up and the conversation will fizzle out. Once you have obtained a detail you can confirm and test the detail by using closed questions.

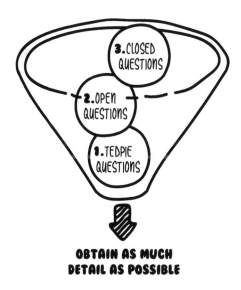

OBTAIN AS MUCH DETAIL AS POSSIBLE

The TEDPIE funnel

COMMUNICATION TASK: USING FUNNELLING

Practise funnelling on your friends and family using a combination of the question types; you have already written down examples of open, closed, and TEDPIE questions in the previous breakouts. Do not forget to use your eyes to help check the responses to your questions and your ears to hear what is being said and not just what you want to hear, or not listening at all.

Summary

Questioning skills are probably among the hardest things to master, as you can so easily close questions down and not gain any new information or detail. Looking back at the definition, a 'conversation' is the sharing of information, ideas, thoughts, and feelings, and you will struggle to do this without asking questions, no matter what the type. Open questions are your best opportunity to seek information about another during a conversation. They can be challenging or probing and, if combined with TEDPIE, could give you more information than you first anticipated; you will then have more avenues to explore and share in your conversation. Using the closed questions will confirm details, and if you are only looking for a short answer or a 'yes' or 'no' answer then these are the ones to use; do not over-use closed questions as this could turn your conversation into a boring question-and-answer session with little if any information, thoughts, or feelings being exchanged.

If you use all of these question types together in the right quantities, you will be amazed at how much you can find out and share during your conversation, making the whole interaction a great experience and a great way to develop an understanding of others while having the opportunity to share and expand your knowledge.

Seek feedback from others about your questioning style or consciously listen to yourself when you are asking questions. Are you asking open or closed questions? Recognising this will help you to avoid asking only closed questions.

In the next section I will get you to think about the knowledge and skills that you already possess, and you will soon realise that you have more than you think.

CHAPTER 7

Knowledge

'*Ipsa scientia potestas est.*' ('Knowledge itself is power.')
  — Francis Bacon

Knowledge is important, and I am not just referring to intellect or Mensa scores. Yes, knowing about history, politics, current affairs, and news is all important and will give you an insight to the current world trends. And yes, you can read and learn about all of this, or at least have an informed opinion about it. But is this really you? Employers, interviewers, universities, and people you meet for the first time are generally interested in *you* and the qualities and strengths that you bring to the table; we can all read and improve our knowledge, but what have you really done with your life so far?

This section will explore how you can identify your knowledge base and how you can use this in conversations. You will find that you do not always have to have the exactly matching personal story or experience to join a conversation or answer a question; many events and stories can be linked in in a looser way – for example, sports, holidays and hobbies are not the same, but they all provide potential for identifying common ground. I will introduce you to the STAR template as a way of remembering and using your knowledge to best effect and using it to demonstrate your evidence in a written application. In this section I will also look at how you can improve your knowledge in preparation for a challenging conversation; for example, knowledge of your rights, your responsibilities, where to get help, and what to expect when getting ready for interviews.

This section will also contain information on why CVs (curriculum vitae) are important and why knowing your evidence inside out is key to targeting the job or further education course that you are after. There will be a task for you to complete to help you identify knowledge that you may not have considered in the past.

What knowledge do you already have?

COMMUNICATION TASK: EXPLORING YOUR KNOWLEDGE

[task sheet – https://www.speakwithinfluence.co.uk/learning-support/]

Before we go any further, I want you to write down all the things that you have done; it does not matter how small you think they are. I have included a template in the 'Learning & Support' tab on my website to get you started and to help you to remember things. Why do I ask you to write them down? Because you will find that as you focus and start to write things down other events and memories will pop into your head – things that you may have even forgotten that you have done; these newly remembered things could all help in starting a conversation or answering an interview question.

You may find it easier to mind-map your knowledge as we discussed in the 'Plan And Prepare' chapter. Whichever way works for you, it is worth spending some time exploring and expanding your 'knowledge'.

So, you now have a list of your 'knowledge', but how can you use this in a conversation or interview? I would imagine that as it stands your knowledge list will not have much structure or mean much to others if you were to mention it in a conversation or interview. To help with this, especially when preparing for an interview or completing an evidence-based application, there is an evidence template that is widely used called STAR. I have used it many times in my career for successful applications, promotion boards, and annual reviews. STAR is designed as a competency-based way of demonstrating your skills and abilities to complete a task. The beauty of STAR is that it gives a simple format for structuring the knowledge that you have so that it means something and showcases your skills and abilities.

'Situation' forms an introduction, describing the scenario you were in, including the time and place. This should only represent 10% of your evidence.

'Task' outlines your role in the situation and the goal that you had to achieve. This should also only form 10% of your evidence.

'Action' forms the main body and should be the longest part – 70% of the evidence. Here you should describe what *you* did to complete the task and resolve the situation.

'Result' is the conclusion – what happened? Did you achieve your goal? Even if you were unsuccessful, explain what you learned from the experience. Reflecting on what worked and what did not work is as important as results because this is how you will learn and develop. This final area should be 10% of the evidence.

Below I have provided an example of a completed STAR competency assessment so that you can understand how to structure your own knowledge evidence. You can find other examples by typing 'STAR competency examples' into web browsers.

Of course, there are many ways to display your evidence and to structure it so that you can remember it whenever you need to use or refer to it. I have talked about interviews and work-based assessments, but if you are in a different type of conversation you can still include elements from your evidence because you have structured it and it makes sense. Have a go at bringing your 'knowledge' into conversations at an appropriate time, or start off a conversation by introducing a situation that you found yourself in. You can make it fun, dramatic, or light hearted, just remember to be confident and let others join in your conversation and share their experiences too. This is where you can also practise your tone of voice and body language to emphasise or highlight a point in your 'story'.

S – During the summer I worked in a local supermarket to improve my customer service skills.

T – My role was to ensure that fresh fruit and vegetables were kept replenished and any poor-quality produce was removed from the displays.

A – To achieve this: At the start of each shift I checked the delivery of fresh produce

- I ensured that it was stored correctly to maintain its quality and freshness

- If not, I would take responsibility for moving it to the cold store as soon as possible; this prevented loss of revenue for the store, and customers had the best quality produce to choose from

- I ensured that displays were stocked and replenished as required

- I checked the quality of produce and removed any not up to standard; I also sought guidance to arrange the disposal or reduction in price of this produce

- I spoke with customers looking for products and directed them to their location or sought advice from colleagues with better knowledge of the product range

- If customers had a problem or complaint about the produce I listened to their concern and did my best to resolve their issue by explaining why the produce they wanted was not available or checking to locate any fresh stock

R – Working at the supermarket improved my confidence in speaking and in managing difficult and challenging conversations with colleagues and customers; it also improved my problem-solving skills. I have gained an understanding of retail, which I can build on in my future studies and work experiences.

COMMUNICATION TASK: WRITING STAR COMPETENCY EXAMPLES

Below are several questions that you may be asked in an interview. Using the STAR competency model, I would like you to think of examples from your own knowledge and experience to produce a set of clear and comprehensive situations for you to use as evidence. Try and limit your word count to 200 words as this is generally the excepted amount required by recruiters for each example of your competence. The word limit also makes you keep your replies focused and to the point with no waffle!

- Describe a major challenge or problem that you have faced. How did you handle it?
- Describe a situation where you have worked as part of a team to achieve something
- Describe an example of a situation where you had to deal with conflict
- How do you deal with working under pressure?
- When did you work the hardest and feel the greatest sense of achievement?

Do not forget that you can always improve or expand your knowledge by spending time researching the things that motivate you or push your boundaries by seeking new adventures or interests. Watch the news, follow people that inspire you on social media – there are a multitude of ways to learn. Challenge yourself to find out something new every day. It does not have to be a major thing; it could be something like learning a new word and its meaning or a new definition – it all expands your knowledge.

You could set yourself daily or weekly goals to learn something new or to speak to someone new so that you can practise and improve your networking and conversation skills. Do not procrastinate; just give it a go and don't be put off if you do not quite get it right the first time. Just keep on trying; you will succeed, and you will become better.

CVs

Why are your CV (curriculum vitae), appraisal form, letter of introduction, or application so important? They offer an insight about you to your employer, future employer, or college/university. Apart from just answering questions or filling boxes they will want to see you in the words you write or the evidence you give. Yes, they want to see a well-written and well-laid-out résumé, but they also want to find out more about you. Will you fit into the team, will you get along with people, are you willing to learn and explore? These are all things that you can incorporate into your CV without writing an inordinately long piece of work.

Quite often your résumé or CV will be limited to a certain number of words; this gives everyone the same chance to sell themselves, but it also means that the person reading your résumé does not have to spend days and days going through all the applications. 'Great,' I hear you say, 'now I am restricted on words!' This is good news, although you may not think it now; being given a set number of words means that you will have to be concise in your evidence. You must therefore look at the questions and then at your evidence to determine which piece of your evidence most closely fits the requirements. Do not waffle or cut down your evidence so that it makes no sense. Sometimes you will be able to use bullet points, but it is best to use a combination of bullets and description. If you write up your evidence as I have shown above using STAR, it will make much more sense and is easy for the reader to see what *you* have done. Remember, this is your evidence, so you must use 'I' and not 'we'. Too much 'we' and it may look like you were not the lead in your evidence.

You have now been shortlisted and are attending an interview; this may be face-to-face, by telephone, or via Skype; whichever format this takes it is likely that you will be asked about your evidence and expected to expand on the detail. This is where you will be found out if it is not your evidence or if you have made some of it up. Again, this is where STAR helps as it lays out your evidence logically and clearly. This should help you to remember it if you have taken the time before the interview to review it. It is amazing how quickly you will forget little things if you do not revisit your evidence on a regular basis.

While I am talking about CVs, please do not use the same CV for everything! Not every job or application is the same. There will be differences, even if they are subtle, so adapt your CV to suit. The core elements of your CV, like education, will stay the same, but your evidence may need to change to suit the expectation of the organisation you are sending your CV to.

What other knowledge do you need?

By now you should have a good idea of all the knowledge that you already have from the tasks that I have set. But what other knowledge is it good to have? Over the next few paragraphs I will outline other knowledge that will be useful for you to have and find out more about. As the opening quote to this chapter says, knowledge is power.

Legal rights

Everyone has rights, and this includes every child and young person, and these are protected by law. But how many of you actually know about your own rights and the rights of others? There are so many different rights depending on what you are doing that I couldn't possibly cover them in this chapter; it would take a whole book to go through them all. The rights that you should be most familiar with are those set out in the Universal Declaration of Human Rights 1948, the European Convention on Human Rights, The Human Rights Act 1988, the Employment Rights Act 1996, and the Equality Act 2010. You will find that the rights in these pieces of legislation will cover many of the issues and challenges that you may face as you start your new careers or further education, and you as well as other job-seekers, students, and employers are bound by these laws. Legislation is always being amended, so make sure you are up to date with the latest versions.

Moral rights

The above examples are just a few of the legal rights in the UK, but there are also another set of rights – moral rights, or shall we call them 'politeness and courteous rights' – stating that we can all respect one another, be polite, and treat others in a thoughtful and courteous way. These rights are standards that are expected within society; some are founded on religious writings, others from common law which have never been formally written down, or expectations of our parents and their parents which have been passed down through generations. You may not agree with some of these moral rights, but be aware of them and acknowledge that others may hold these rights as their core values and beliefs, and they can find it difficult to relate to others who do not hold the same beliefs or values.

Responsibilities

You now have some knowledge about your rights, but you also need to know about your responsibilities, whether at school, college, university, work, or in everyday life. Personal responsibility means that you need to be accountable for your own actions or mistakes. If you do not take personal responsibility, it can have a harmful influence on your future success. It is important not to blame others for your lack of success but to be honest with yourself and reflect on why you have not achieved; was it lack of focus or preparation or procrastination that has led to your current situation? Once you have taken responsibility you can then do something about it and move forward to achieving those successes. This is where you will gain your knowledge about yourself and how you react to situations: do you blame others, look for excuses – or reflect, change, and move on? Schools, colleges, universities and employers will want to see evidence that you are able to take personal responsibility for your own actions and to learn from your mistakes, so make sure that you include this in any résumé or personal profile that you complete or have to submit.

Finding help about your rights

Finding help to improve your knowledge of your legal rights is straightforward, especially using the government websites for information on the legislation. You will find that summaries are available under explanatory notes if you are just looking for an overview of the legislation you are interested in. Other help can be found from libraries, local citizen advice centres, or local government departments. Finding information about moral rights can be a little more challenging because they may vary depending on culture and background. Speak to your parents and family members, and ask different people from diverse backgrounds about what they expect from you or others as a sign of respect or consideration of their beliefs.

Knowledge tips for interviews

Interviews come in a variety of formats. Make sure you know which type of interview you are attending. Remember, no two interviews will be the same!

In formal or structured interviews, the questions are asked in a consistent order and the interviewer will not move away from the interview agenda or prompt you beyond the answers that you give. In an informal unstructured interview, the questions are not structured and do follow a set agenda, and this gives the interviewer the chance to search for a clearer understanding or seek clarification. It also allows you to steer the direction of the interview. These types of interviews are held as 'discovery' meetings to find out more about you in an informal setting such as a coffee shop.

In a group interview, you and other applicants may be interviewed simultaneously. In this setting, the interviewer may ask you each to answer the same questions or ask each of you different questions. Sometimes you will be asked to solve a problem as a team or to hold a discussion or debate on a topic chosen by the interviewer.

Job interviews

Your interview may take place anywhere, but generally it will take place at the company's office if you are applying for a job or at an educational establishment if applying for a course. Once you arrive, you may be asked to wait until the interviewer is ready to see you. Most job interviews are one-on-one interviews with the team leader for whom you would be working. Occasionally you will be interviewed by a panel of interviewers, including a member of the human resources division.

The interview may begin with information about the job or the company, or general questions to make you feel at ease, but the main part of the interview consist of specific questions that assess whether you will fit well into the company and appraise your general behaviour and skills. The following are the types of questions you might encounter.

Verification questions: These questions will require you to provide unbiased information about yourself;

for example, your qualifications and employment history. You may have already provided this, in which case the interviewer is checking the facts on your application.

Competency/behavioural questions: the interviewer may ask you to describe a situation when you demonstrated a particular quality. Remember STAR earlier in the chapter. These questions indicate how you may handle similar situations in a new job or role.

Situational questions: This is where the interviewer describes a situation and asks you to explain how you would approach and deal with it. This is intended to gauge how you may handle situations that may arise in the workplace.

Once the interviewer has finished asking you questions, you will be asked if you have any questions of your own. This is a chance for you to ask any questions that you may have and to demonstrate that you have done your homework about the job or role and are genuinely interested in the company. Be comfortable asking questions and check that the role and company are right for you.

Do not expect to be told that you definitively have or do not have the job at the interview. If you have not already been told when you will hear an answer, ask before you leave. Remember that no interview is a waste of your time, even if you did not get the job or you decided it was not for you. Every interview offers an opportunity to practise your interview skills and to decide what types of jobs and organisations best fit your personality, interests, and skills.

University or college interviews

Once you have successfully submitted your personal statement you will be invited for interview. Most colleges and higher education establishments hold structured traditional interviews to find out whether you are a good fit for the course that you are applying for – much the same as a job interview. You will probably find that there will be questions based on your personal qualities and transferable skills as well as what you know about the course. You will need to show that you have identified and considered your strengths or weaknesses and should be able to discuss your current studies. Talk about what you have liked about your studies and what you are looking forward to learning in the future to prepare you for your future career. As identified in the job interview section above, there may be a panel of interviewers or one course lecturer. Whichever type of interview it is, you should prepare to have a comprehensive conversation about yourself.

You can find further help and information on interviews – both for jobs and higher education – on numerous career websites and mobile apps, and from career advisors, to name but a few resources. Also take a look at the 'Resources' section at the back of the book for some more suggestions.

Summary

Your knowledge is about you, who you are, what you have achieved so far, where you have been, and where you want to go. It is also about what you know, your skills, your abilities, your passions, and your dislikes. With your knowledge you will be able to start, join in, or debate with others during conversations. Share your experiences, thoughts, or feelings, and think back to the definition of 'conversation' – knowledge has a large part to play in this.

Knowledge can encompass almost anything you or your future employer, college or university want it to; it all depends on the context, the needs, and the evidence that is required for any subject, course, role, or career. What you must do is explore your own existing knowledge (skills, abilities, experiences, etc) and then be able to present your evidence clearly, concisely, and in a structured way.

STAR is an excellent way to do this. It does take a bit of practise to get it right, but it does explain your evidence from the situation you found yourself in through what you had to do, how and why you did something to resolve the situation, and what the outcome was. Writing and remembering your evidence like this will help you at interviews or appraisals, and you will already have structure and the evidence of what *you* did.

You will have identified much of your current knowledge to use as evidence, but I have also introduced to you the need to find out more about your rights and the rights of others and to consider the moral rights and the responsibilities expected of you by your society. These in themselves will expand your personal knowledge and help you to explore different cultures and tolerate others' beliefs.

I have introduced interviews in this section to give you a quick overview of an important topic. Interviews are part of your future, whether you pursue a course in higher education or whether starting out on a new career path, and they will all be different. Take your time to plan and prepare for those interviews, and make sure that you give yourself the best opportunity to answer the questions, whether in a structured formal interview or an informal interview to find out about you.

Use your knowledge, expand your knowledge, and remember your knowledge, and not only will you be able to start a conversation but you will be able to join conversations and debates and also be prepared for appraisals, interviews, CVs, and applications. No matter what your age, there is always time to learn something new.

PART THREE
SAMPLE CONVERSATIONS

Introduction: Putting It All Together

'It was impossible to get a conversation going;
everybody was talking too much.'
— **Yogi Berra**

Let us start by revisiting and breaking down the
definition of 'conversation' and recap what you have
learned through the process:

A 'talk between two or more people': You are one
of these people, so unless you are doing a mono-
logue or dictating to a piece of technology you are
having a conversation as soon as you communicate
with someone else. Even comments to a blog post or

tweet is seeking to start a conversation, whether it is to search for likeminded people or to obtain some sort of reaction from those who are not entirely on the same wavelength (or planet, as it sometimes seems!) as you. As you have seen, there are over 5,000 different ways to communicate with someone, so it is vital that you understand the pluses and minuses of the method that you are using to avoid your message being misunderstood or ignored or causing conflict.

'... thoughts, feelings, and ideas are expressed...': Preparation comes in here so that you understand who you will talking to, the context of the conversation, and what will be acceptable in the given situation. It will not help expressing your disgust with a subject to someone who is passionate about that issue. That is not to say that you cannot discuss the subject, but you must each be open to feedback and empathic to the other's view.

'... questions are asked and answered...': This sums up both the 'E' and 'A' of SPEAK. If you do not hear the question, you cannot answer it; if you do not ask questions, you will not get an answer. The better the question, the better the answer and the better the conversation.

'... news and information is exchanged...': This is where your knowledge comes into its own. Your skills, experiences, interests, and research will allow you to exchange and share information with others to have a great and fulfilling conversations.

Having said all of this, holding a conversation is a skill, and you will need to practise perfecting that skill. So, do not rush it; take your time and start with the simple stuff like talking to your friends and getting a good conversation or debate going. As I said right at the beginning of this book, there are lots of ways to hold a conversation, so if social media is your thing then this is where you start. Remember, though, that your message must be clear and understood by the person you are sending it to, otherwise the conversation will fail or at the very least you will be misunderstood.

Start with one of those great open descriptive questions from TEDPIE to get things going. Do not forget to listen to the reply so that you can ask further open questions to explore a little more. Conversations are two-way, so share a little of yourself, otherwise it will sound just like an interrogation and that is not what conversations with friends and family are about. Even in police interviews there are questions and answers, even if it is a 'no comment' interview. Remember that there are often many differing views on any subject discussed or debated, and you must be open and accepting to another's opinion – but they should also be open to yours.

Look back at the conversation styles discussed earlier in the book; which one was yours? You can change your styles or have a combination; however, the assertive style is the best and most effective to support genuine conversations that are supportive, informative, and fulfilling. Everyone involved has a win–win outcome, learning and sharing and feeling part of that conversation.

In the final chapter we're going to have a look at some challenging conversations you may have.

CHAPTER 8

Conversation Cases

'The real art of conversation is not only to say the right thing at the right place but to leave unsaid the wrong thing at the tempting moment.'
— **Dorothy Nevill**

In this section we're going to have a look at examples of the different types of conversation you may find yourself facing. While no two conversations will be the same and the way you approach the subject must be unique to any given conversation, I'll set out why the conversation matters, ways to prepare, and why it's important that you find the courage to speak up.

Bullying At School

One of the most common situations young people face today involves dealing with a school bully. This may be a one-off occurrence, or it can go on for a long time, but bullying in any form is unkind and can make someone's life unhappy. No one deserves to be bullied.

Who you should talk to: Decide who is the best person to help you. If you need advice or moral support, a trusted friend can be perfect. If you want help getting bullying to stop, then speak to a teacher or your parents. If you feel confident and you're not at risk, speak to the bully.

What you might say: Be brave and tell people what's happening – use simple language, such as: 'I am being bullied. I am being pushed around, called names, and being treated as if I do not have any rights or even exist. I am constantly being targeted on social media and by text. I feel depressed, worthless and useless, and feel that I am powerless to prevent this continuing. Will it ever stop?'

When you should have this conversation: This conversation usually happens when things have got so bad that the situation is causing stress and anxiety, and affecting your education, social life and home life. Don't wait that long; have the conversation earlier if possible.

Why this conversation is challenging: Speaking about the problem may make you feel that you are not strong enough or good enough to face the bullies. You may also feel that your peers will look at you as some kind of 'tell-tale' or trouble maker.

What will happen if you don't have the conversation: You may continue to experience stress, anxiety, and other challenges to your emotional wellbeing. Bullying may have an impact on your education, if you are now not turning up for lessons. Your social life with friends could become non-existent if you are afraid you will meet your tormentors outside of school. You might become withdrawn at home if you are afraid of the reaction from your parents to the drop in your school attendance or results. This could lead to depression or worse.

What will happen if you do have the conversation: Having a conversation when the bullying is just starting will empower you to express how it is affecting you. Verbalising this to a trusted teacher, peer, or parents will give you the strength to seek help, guidance, and a resolution to the bullying. This will help to prevent you feeling weak or powerless and being afraid of what others think. Your studies will not suffer further, and, if they have suffered already, having the conversation will help others to realise why this happened and to adjust your learning to get you back on track. You will feel stronger and more confident about challenging others in the future. You will also find that you are the spokesperson for others who are suffering bullying.

Even if the bullying stops immediately, you may continue to feel anxious, upset or even angry about what has happened to you. It may take time for you to process what has happened to you, so remember to keep talking about how you are feeling and how the experience may have affected you.

How to do it well: There are many ways of dealing with bullies: for example, you could seek guidance and advice from the internet. But don't do nothing or hope that they will leave you alone and go away. In most cases they won't, and the bullying will get worse if they realise that you are just 'taking it' or it is making you upset. This is how bullies get their kicks; it only serves to make them feel stronger, and they will continue to torment you and start on others.

The best way to start is to talk to a trusted friend – someone who you know will take the time to listen to you and not interrupt. Plan how the conversation with your friend will go; you need to structure it to ensure that you get all the worries and concerns that you have out in the open. Don't bottle anything up, as mulling over particular details and regretting not mentioning them during the conversation will only lead to your anxiety, stress, and worries continuing. Start by telling your friend what the general problem is (ie, 'I am being bullied by Jim'), and explain when and how this is happening. Tell them how this is making you feel and how it is affecting your studies and other aspects of your life.

Your friend may have also experienced the same thing or know someone who has. They may be able to tell you how they dealt with it and the action they took. They may not feel they are able to help you deal with the bullies, but by listening to you they will have made a big difference to how you are feeling. If you have spoken to a friend, you are now able to speak to a trusted teacher or your parents.

There are of course many organisations and support groups that can help and support you.

Educational Failures

This conversation is becoming more prevalent as acceptance of different learning styles and educational difficulties improves. We can all have good and bad days at school, but, for some of us, learning and studying in an educational environment can be complex and overwhelming.

Who you should talk to: This is a conversation you could have with your parents, teachers, careers advisors, and – frequently – yourself.

What you might say: Frequently this conversation, whether in your own head or out loud to an important adult in your life, goes along the lines of: 'I really struggled at school and had difficulty understanding, but instead of seeking help I acted the clown and played truant. I have left school with poor grades and feel that I will never be able to get a good job or worthwhile career. I am a loser!'

When you should have this conversation: This conversation may have started long ago, with the realisation that studying and absorbing information in the classroom were increasingly difficult, but you kept saying to yourself that things would work out. Instead of speaking up about your problems you avoided the subject, and may have begun to act the fool and avoid lessons to stop yourself feeling stupid and being regarded by others as a failure. While you can't go back and change the past, now is the best time to have this conversation and see what you can do for the future.

Why this conversation is challenging: To admit that you are struggling becomes more and more of a challenge if you know that you should have spoken about it to someone earlier. You may feel it is increasingly difficult to verbalise the problems you are having because you have done a really good job of avoiding and ignoring them, or even making excuses for your difficulties.

What will happen if you don't have the conversation: If you do not recognise your difficulties and put them into words, no one will be able to help you. You could end up unemployable because you have started mixing with others who do not care about getting a good job or career, and would rather get paid for doing little or nothing. You could end up as an alcoholic or substance abuser, lose your family, friends, and even your life. Your future depends on your honesty with yourself and people who can help you.

What will happen if you do have the conversation: Difficulties in education and learning have been recognised as needing more attention, so that young people can be supported in their development. There are now many opportunities and courses available for those who have struggled at school. By seeking help you will discover opportunities for further education that can be tailored to your learning style, with teachers and lecturers who understand your needs. This will give you the confidence to gain qualifications and believe in your abilities, with the real chance of the career and future you have always dreamed of. It's not too late.

How to do it well: As soon as you recognise that you are having difficulty with a subject, you need to speak to a supportive teacher or someone within the school who you feel you could talk to. It may be that you have a pastoral care member of staff who will listen to you in confidence. Don't try to hide the fact that you are struggling by creating a smokescreen to deflect attention from the issue. This will only cause you more problems in the long run, for example, being excluded, playing truant, or being considered the fool or the class clown.

Make a note of the subjects that you are struggling with and record exactly which part is causing the concern: it could be writing, numbers, spelling, etc. Once you have a clear idea of what you are struggling with you should approach your form tutor or that trusted person – it may even be a parent – and tell them exactly what the problem is. Use your notes and do not leave anything out. Tell them how it is making you feel and state your concerns for the future. By doing this you are taking responsibility for your learning and will gain support for your future. Do not let your struggles become a lead weight tied to your feet.

New School, College, Or Job

We all have conversations on this topic: education and employment changes may recur throughout your life, so getting good at having these conversations is a useful life skill.

Who you should talk to: You'll probably want to give yourself a pep talk. You can also speak to your parents and friends who may also be facing the same issues.

What you might be feeling and thinking: 'I am scared, worried, and anxious about starting somewhere new and unfamiliar. I will have to meet new people and start to establish myself all over again. What if I don't get on with others or they do not like me? What if I don't fit in? What if...? What if...?'

When you should have this conversation: The conversation with yourself will probably start at quite an early stage, even before the change. The worries, doubts, and fears will niggle away at you and keep popping into your head. You may try to talk to your family and friends, but it never comes out right and you feel you are getting anxious about nothing. Persevere – you have nothing to lose.

Why this conversation is challenging: Change can be unsettling because, as humans, we like to have routine, to feel safe and secure, to be sure of our surroundings, and to be liked. When you must change your surroundings and start again somewhere new, you may feel anxious and fearful of what lies ahead. You will have doubts about why you are making this change: sometimes you will have no choice, as you are starting at college or university or your family have moved to a new location for employment, financial, or health reasons. New surroundings, new friends, new subjects to study, and probably a new set of rules to follow can be daunting, and admitting to this can make you feel weak or out of control.

What will happen if you don't have the conversation: It is only natural to be afraid of change, but the worst thing that you can do is refuse to move forward. By not moving forward you will try and hang on to the past, and you will stop evolving and developing your skills and experiences. You will find that everyone around you will be moving on and away, exploring the world around them, and you will be left in the past, afraid to leave your comfort and security. The effect of this is that you will not reach your full potential, and you will end up in a job that is safe but not satisfying. You may miss out on opportunities to travel and meet new people who can help you achieve the future you want and deserve.

What will happen if you do have the conversation: Fear of change is something that most people experience. It does take courage to admit that you are afraid of change and acknowledge the things that are worrying you. By exploring your fears, you will become better at dealing with change, and, in the future, you will find it much easier to accept that you are going to have these worries and concerns, but that you can overcome them and work through them, leading to a more positive experience of change.

How to do it well: Before you can deal with your worries and concerns you must first admit to yourself how you are feeling and why. You must be honest with yourself; don't feel that you are being silly or stupid. It's OK to be afraid of new beginnings and new challenges, but don't let them control you or stop you from doing something. You will only regret it in the future and wish that you had taken that step into the unknown.

Once you have admitted your fears to yourself then you can do something about changing that negative feeling into a positive experience. You can help yourself by writing down your worries and concerns in one column and in a facing column listing all the advantages and experiences that will come from the move or change. Don't just think of the negatives, really explore all the positives. Once you have your lists, discuss with your friends and family how you are feeling and why you are anxious about the change. Be honest with them and ask them what they have done to help overcome any similar worries in the past.

Research the place where you are going and arrange to visit. All this will start to make you feel more comfortable about the change and your new surroundings. Before long, you will feel like you have always been there. Talk to other people you meet and you will find that they have had the same fears as you. Explore these feelings together and find ways to overcome them by joining clubs and societies and visiting new places. Turn your negatives into positives.

Mental Health

Stress, anxiety, and depression

Many people, at some time in their lives, will have to cope with emotions that challenge their mental health. Problems can arise from any number of stresses: relationships, school or job stress, or money worries. It's nothing to be ashamed of. This can be a natural response to the problems that we are facing. Mostly, with time, adjustments we make to our lives, and the support of those around us, these feelings go away or we learn to manage them successfully and lead fulfilling lives.

Who you should talk to: Depression, anxiety and stress can affect anyone at any time, and you deserve help to feel better. If you feel able to, talk to someone you like and trust, for example, a teacher, close relative, counsellor or good friend.

You should also speak to your doctor, as they may offer to refer you to one of the many mental health support agencies or to an experienced professional who can help you. If you feel that you are not ready for a face-to-face conversation, then you can speak to online advisors who can give you support and advice. What you must avoid is keeping it all inside your head: speak about your problems out loud.

What you might be feeling and thinking: Mild depression can just mean that you are feeling in low spirits and some things in your normal routine are becoming harder to carry out and seem less meaningful, but depression can also be life-threatening: at its most severe you may feel that you just want to give up on life.

You may feel that a great big black cloud is constantly above your head, making things dark and lonely; everywhere you go the black cloud seems to follow you.

You may be feeling upset and angry for no apparent reason. You may be tearful and not sleeping well, or continually worrying. You may be telling yourself that you are not good enough and putting yourself down. If your self-confidence or self-esteem has taken a real knock, you may make excuses not to go out, preferring to shut yourself away.

When you should have this conversation: There are many signs and symptoms of depression, anxiety and stress, but everyone's experience will vary, and it is important to recognise when your low spirits are beginning to interfere with your ability to manage your day-to-day routine. If you can see this happening, you need to start seeking that conversation with a trusted person, doctor or online advisor. The sooner you have the conversation the sooner you can get the help you need to lead a bright and happy life.

Why this conversation is challenging: It can be difficult to talk about your feelings or problems with family, friends or partners as you may be worried about upsetting the people who care about you, or about how it might affect your relationship with them.

Even if you come across advertisements about support for those with mental health issues, they always feel as if they are aimed at other people, not at you. You may try to deal with the depression, stress or anxiety yourself, as you feel that no one else will understand. You may tell yourself that everything is OK, and it is just a temporary thing and will go away. You are afraid of the labels 'mental health', 'stress', 'anxiety' or 'depression' and will do everything not to be marked with these labels.

What will happen if you don't have the conversation: The problem will not go away. It might feel as if it does some of the time, as things change around you, but it will still be there and will raise its head again sometime in the future, when you least expect it. Mental health concerns can be very debilitating and stop you from doing things. You can become a recluse, afraid to go out, or you may even stop talking to friends and family. You might even resort to recreational drugs or drink to give you stability when you are feeling particularly low, but these will only add to your mental health problems and may even make them worse. Ultimately, your stress and anxiety may become depression, which at its most severe may make you feel that life is not worth the struggle.

What will happen if you do have the conversation: Mental health issues are not stigmatised as they once were and are much more common than you might expect – especially with today's hectic and pressured lifestyles.

Dealing with depression can make it hard to find the energy to look after yourself, but by taking an active role in your treatment and taking steps to help yourself tackle the causes, you can – with the help and support of others –lessen its impact on your life. Medication can sometimes be helpful, but it is only to help regulate the chemicals in your brain, and is not necessarily a lifetime prescription.

By seeking help to recognise what is causing the problem, and finding a way to manage it, you will find that you are better able to cope with the symptoms of your depression, anxiety or stress. Chatting to family and friends or your GP to express how you are feeling on any particular day, being honest with yourself about how you are feeling, and confronting the areas that are responsible for your depression – all these will help you manage to live life and achieve your goals without worrying that your mental health might get in the way.

How to do it well: There are several theories about the causes of depression, and the causes vary from person to person. Some people find that they become depressed for no obvious reason, whereas other people's depression may be linked to a stressful or traumatic event, for example bereavement, losing your job, moving home or getting married.

The first thing is to recognise when things are getting too much. Are you feeling anxious, worried, or do you feel like running away or giving up? The hardest part is to accept that this is happening to you – especially if you are normally able to deal with most things.

Once you accept the fact that you are feeling this way, you should speak to someone that you trust and that you feel will listen to you. Quite often the best person to see is your doctor, as they will understand your concerns. Before you go, though, make a note of how you are feeling and when you feel like this. Are you sleeping well? Are you finding it difficult to socialise with friends? Or is it the reverse – are you out all the time and drinking more than you did before?

Be honest with the doctor, as they can only give you advice on the basis of what you tell them. If you do not tell them everything, their capacity to help will be limited. Answer their questions honestly and don't hide things because you think they will think that you are wasting their time. Mental ill health can be a life-threatening condition if not treated seriously and appropriately.

If you feel more comfortable opening up to your friends or family, then it may help if you use the communication method you feel most comfortable with in the first instance. This could be face-to-face, on the phone or in a letter. The people closest to you are often the greatest source of support in working through your depression, anxiety or stress-related illness.

It is important to realise that the first conversation you have may not solve all your problems at once, as understanding mental health problems can take time. Your friends and family may be shocked or react badly at first, and you will need to give them time to take in what you have told them. Do not give up if this is the reaction at first; if possible, revisit your conversation with them, so that you are able to explain exactly what you're going through.

There are of course many organisations and support groups that will also help and support you, which I have listed in the 'Resources' section at the back of the book.

Suicidal thoughts

Anyone may have suicidal thoughts at some point in their life, whatever their background or situation.

There is a wide range of possible causes, including an existing mental health problem. Suicidal thoughts can range from feeling that people would be better off without you or being fixated by hypothetical thoughts about ending your life, to researching methods of suicide or making clear plans to take your own life.

For young people life can be emotionally turbulent, as they have to deal with the changes associated with their physical and emotional development. Exploring the options for their future and striving to succeed and to fit in can also be stressful.

Who you should talk to: If you are feeling suicidal or having suicidal thoughts, then talking to someone who will listen and be supportive may be your first step toward getting help.

You could talk to someone in your life, such as a family member or partner, or to a professional, such as a doctor or counsellor. There are many telephone and online crisis helplines that have trained operators who will listen and be non-judgemental, and will support you and provide you with information.

There are also telephone and online peer support groups you can contact where people have had similar experiences, so you can share your thoughts and receive tips for coping from others who understand what you are going through.

If you are feeling that you cannot keep yourself safe right now, seek immediate help. You can go to any hospital A&E department or call – or get someone else to call – 999 and ask for an ambulance if you can't get to A&E.

What you might be feeling and thinking: Everyone's experience of suicidal thoughts will be unique to them. You may not know or understand why you are feeling the way you are feeling, but you just know that everything is hopeless and there is no point in living.

You may be tearful and overwhelmed by harmful thoughts and feel as if you have an intolerable pain that you believe will never end. You may feel useless, unwanted or cast off by others and think that everyone would be better off without you. At times you feel as if you are cut off from your body or are physically numb and as though you are in a deep, dark pit that you cannot escape from.

You may be thinking things like: 'I just don't want to go on.' 'It would be better for everyone if I just ended it.' 'I hate my life.' 'I miss them so much; I just want to be with them.' 'I can't go on without them.'

When you should have this conversation: You may find it hard to tell others how you are feeling but the earlier you are able to let someone know how you're feeling, the quicker you'll be able to get help and support to overcome these feelings.

Why this conversation is challenging: There may be many reasons why you would find this conversation challenging: you may be feeling that you do not have any friends and are cut off from everyone and everything. You may be finding it difficult to admit you are having problems that you are unable to solve. You may not want to accept that you have not yet reached a goal or target and be unable to cope with this disappointment.

Although you may want others to understand what you're going through, you may be unsure of who to tell for fear that they will not understand or that they may judge you, or that you will upset those close to you.

What will happen if you don't have the conversation: If you do not share your feelings with others, you might find it even harder to believe that there could be a solution to your pain. You could become preoccupied with suicidal thoughts, and this might make them even stronger. if you then focus on all the hopelessness negative thoughts about being a burden and of no use to anyone, this could become overwhelming, and you would see no other way out but to take your own life.

What will happen if you do have the conversation:
It's important to remember that you are not alone: support is available from a multitude of sources, so always ask for help. Talking can be hard, but it can help you through the times of hopelessness and pain.

If you're thinking of harming yourself, you need to find a coping technique that works for you: for example, you could sit somewhere comfortable, somewhere that you feel is a safe place, and write down how you're feeling; you could reach out and talk to someone you know who you feel would be supportive and listen to you. You could contact a helpline or peer support group.

Having a conversation, be it with yourself, family, friends, a GP or a support network about how you are feeling, or focusing on something real will make it easier for you to deal with and face down the feelings of hopelessness.

Talking to your GP is a good starting point as they will be used to listening to people who are experiencing difficult feelings and they can refer you for talking treatments or specialist services. They may also prescribe medication to help you cope with your problems.

Having a conversation about your feelings with a trained professional, such as a counsellor or mental health professional, can help you to understand why you're experiencing suicidal feelings and to find ways you can help yourself to cope with and resolve the problems that are making you feel that way.

How to do it well: You might be feeling so upset, angry and in pain, and experiencing a sense of extreme hopelessness that has you believing that these feelings will never end. But it's important for you to remember that these feelings cannot and will not last; like all feelings, they will pass. Don't blame yourself for feeling this way; try to accept that this is just how you are feeling at this time. Now you need to focus your energy on looking after yourself.

There are actions that you can take right now to stop yourself from acting on your suicidal thoughts. Everyone is different, so it's about finding which action works best for you. You may find that you must talk to yourself and challenge the way that you are thinking: make a deal with yourself to get through the next five minutes and then the next and so on, rewarding yourself with something that makes you feel good after each five minutes. You could also make a deal with yourself that you will not act on your suicidal thoughts today and distract yourself by writing down the things you are looking forward to, for example, catching up with family or your favourite TV show.

Express your feelings to a friend, family member or even a pet: speaking about how you are feeling can help you to feel less alone and more in control of those feelings. You could even talk to yourself and have a conversation as though you were talking to a good friend. You may think that some of these ideas may seem silly, but it can be easy to forget to do something nice for yourself when you are feeling lost and alone.

You must do whatever you think might help you to get past these thoughts and tell yourself that you can do it, which can help you to regain hope and focus on getting through a difficult time.

Remember that there are many sources of support and help; you do not have to deal with your thoughts and problems alone. In the 'Resources' section of this book I have included a number of these organisations, but there are many more that you might find it easier to approach.

Binge Drinking And Risky Behaviour

Binge drinking usually refers to drinking lots of alcohol in a short space of time, or drinking to get drunk, and it is often instigated at the end of the week when friends meet up at an after-work get-together or a party. Sometimes it just reflects curiosity or peer pressure to try alcohol for the first time or to be part of the 'gang' and keep up with the more experienced drinkers; at other times binge drinking is intended to relieve stress or the pressures of work or study.

Why have I included binge drinking under mental health? Because binge drinking affects the brain and its function, and can therefore affect mood, motivation, memory, learning and attention, and hence your performance at school or college. Binge drinking over time may lead to alcoholism or cirrhosis.

Who you should talk to: If you have a problem with binge drinking or other substance misuse you will probably need to speak to friends and family first. If you are in crisis, though, you may also need to call the emergency services.

What you might be feeling and thinking: You will probably find yourself saying things like: 'It's happy hour!', 'It's just a quick drink', 'Go on, try it – you will like it', 'Drinking helps me to relax or deal with my problems', or 'It helps to drown my sorrows'.

When you should have this conversation: The conversation will probably not happen until the drinking or the behaviour becomes a problem and you have been involved in some sort of incident, hurt yourself or someone else, or suddenly realised what is happening in your life. This realisation may dawn on you at hospital, at the police station, or even back home when you have tried to be quiet letting yourself in!

Why this conversation is challenging: The challenge is acknowledging that you may have a problem with binge drinking. The realisation may come from others around you at first, and you may think that they are overreacting, but listen to what they have to say and reflect on their words and comments. Is this the first time, or have there been others? Do you remember what you did? How did you get home? There are so many questions you could ask yourself about a recent night out, and you need to think about whether this is in character for you and about how you wish to be seen.

You may feel that you must drink to keep your friends, or to be social and be part of the 'in-crowd'; you may even fear missing out on the antics that take place when you are all drunk. Most people enjoy a drink or two but drinking excessively in a short space of time because it is happy hour and you are saving money, or because you are trying to keep up with friends, or even because you are racing the shots is probably not the way to have a good evening!

What will happen if you don't have the conversation: If you do not realise that you are binge drinking or refuse to listen to your friends and family, then you are likely to cut yourself off from the people in your life. You risk becoming isolated from your true friends and ending up with the 'gang', drinking to excess and probably becoming totally reliant on alcohol to manage your life. You will more than likely become a secret drinker, hiding alcohol around the house for a swift tipple at any time. Even worse, you could lose everything and end up as an alcoholic on the streets, sleeping in shelters or in shop doorways.

Binge drinking can lead to several problems, including:

- Having an accident resulting in an injury or, in some cases, causing death

- Misjudging situations, believing you can do something when, if you were sober, you would not even attempt it

- Losing your self-control and getting into trouble by committing criminal offences or having unprotected sex

- Alcohol poisoning, which can lead to seizures, vomiting (which you can choke on), confusion and irregular breathing

- Weight problems and high blood pressure, because of the number of calories in each drink

- Disrupted sleep, which makes it harder to stay awake and concentrate during the day – you may then find yourself struggling with your studies or while at work

- Personality changes: you might become angry or moody while drinking, rather than the fun person you were expecting to be

- Ultimately, if binge drinking becomes a regular occurrence, you may find you cannot live without alcohol and become an alcoholic

These risks are very real if you do not seek help or listen to the feedback that you are being given. You could end up with organ failure, mental health problems, or even have an accident, all of which have the potential to kill you.

What will happen if you do have the conversation:
If you have received feedback from friends and family, you have found yourself feeling poorly, or you have put yourself in dangerous positions and you are feeling out of control when you are socialising, it is time to re-evaluate your alcohol intake. The good news is that there is a lot you can do yourself to manage your binge drinking, but you need to give yourself a good talking-to and promise yourself that you will take action.

Just changing your habits of alcohol consumption will help. You don't have to shut yourself away or refuse to go out; you just need to extend the time it takes you to drink your drink. Once you start to have that conversation with yourself or with friends and family and you start to change your drinking habits, you will be amazed how much better you feel. You will be more in control of yourself, but you will still be able to have a good time out with your friends.

How to do it well: You have had some feedback from your friends about the state you were in last night, or you have seen some social media pictures of you vomiting all over the pavement and then being propped up against a wall while your friend tried to figure out a way of getting you home safe. If this sounds familiar, then you need to be having a serious talk with yourself and your friends about how to avoid this in the future.

Listen to the feedback from your friends and talk with them about the evening; they obviously remember a lot more that you do! By asking open questions you will find out much more about the circumstances of your binge drinking session. What were you drinking? How many did you have? You need to think seriously about what was causing you to drink so much and to assess whether you have other underlying problems like stress or anxiety that you may need to address without getting. If you think that you may do this again, ask your friends to help you by reminding you what you have had to drink. Set yourself a challenge to drink water or a soft drink between each glass or bottle of alcohol and make sure that you have had something to eat before going out. An evening out with friends is supposed to be a chance to relax and unwind, so take your time with each drink.

If you do like to have a few drinks, then make sure that you have planned how you are going to get home. Are you and your friends looking out for each

other, or will you have to make your own way home?
Work this out before you go out and be safe.

See the 'Resources' section at the back of the book for
details of useful organisations.

Relationships And Break-Ups

Relationships make the world go round, but sometimes they bring with them a whole lot of stress and
challenging situations. You may be experiencing the
break-up of a relationship or a crisis in your relationship. We all react in different ways, but it is important
not to let your emotions take control of your rational
behaviour as this can lead to other health problems
such as depression, or drug or alcohol dependence.

Who you should talk to: Depending upon the relationship issue, your first port of call should usually
be talking to yourself, to try to work out where things
have gone wrong and what you should do next.
Getting advice from friends and family can help, and
you of course need to speak to your partner if you
have concerns about something that is affecting your
relationship. You will also find telephone and online
support networks that can help you deal with your
problems.

What you might be feeling and thinking: 'It's all
my fault; I should have been more…', 'I didn't listen',

'I could have done more to keep us together', 'This is not happening, and I refuse to accept it'.

Often in the breakdown of a relationship, whether among family members, friends, or partners, it is common to feel that it is all your fault and to take the blame yourself, making you feel shocked, upset, and, in some cases, distraught and depressed. You may, on the other hand, try to blame others for the failure and develop a dislike or hatred of the person concerned, trying to seek revenge or to undermine them at every opportunity. You may even refuse to accept that there is a problem or that the break-up is happening and try to carry on as normal. Distrust of anyone and everyone is also a common reaction to a breakdown or problem in a relationship, and it can take time to form new relationships or rebuild trust again within the relationship.

When you should have this conversation: With most relationship problems or breakdowns (unless it is you initiating the break-up) the conversation tends to take place after the problem or break-up has happened. The conversation is more likely to take place in reaction to the cause than be planned. However, if you are the one initiating the break-up, you may have spent a considerable amount of time planning how you would tell the other person that you wish to leave them.

If you are having issues within a relationship, you need to keep talking to each other or involve a mediator or someone who will not take sides to help you work through these issues.

Why this conversation is challenging: Relationship issues and break-ups are nothing new, but for you it is likely to be the hardest thing that you will ever have to deal with. Your feelings and emotions will be raw, and you will feel like the bottom has just fallen out of your world. Nothing can prepare you for the range of emotions and the feeling of loss or betrayal in these situations. You will think of nothing else and there are likely be tears alongside the ups and downs of your other emotions –anger, withdrawal, and denial. You may fear that others will talk about you behind your back and make up stories about why the break-up has happened. 'Will it be all over social media? Will I ever be able to face my friends again? Will I be able to trust anyone enough to start another relationship?'

What will happen if you don't have the conversation: If anger and hate take over, you may find yourself doing your utmost to destroy the reputation of the other person. You might stalk them on social media or follow them around. Any of this could lead you to being prosecuted in a criminal court and getting a conviction, which could prevent you from getting the job you had always hoped for or even restrict your travel to other parts of the world.

If you are experiencing problems in your relationship and you refuse to have the conversation with your partner, or even to listen to them, the chances are that your relationship will soon turn sour and end in humiliation. Similarly, if you do not accept and deal with the relationship break-up, you will not feel better. The reasons that you think caused the break-up will just eat away at you, causing you more distress and darkening your mood. As time goes on you may become depressed, and you may start to shut yourself away and no longer be able to face life. You may turn to alcohol or drugs to relieve the pressures and numb your feelings. In extreme circumstances, where the loss has become an all-encompassing focus of your life, you may become depressed or even have suicidal thoughts.

What will happen if you do have the conversation: If you are having problems in your relationship, then having a conversation with your partner about your concerns will relieve some of the tension and give you both the opportunity to explore how you are going to move forward, to either save the relationship or to break up. It is likely to be an emotional conversation, and you may need to involve a third party to help keep you both calm and focused on what you are trying to achieve. Shouting and bellowing at each other will serve no purpose.

If you are experiencing a relationship break-up you may find that having the conversation with yourself or your best friend and admitting to the break-up will help you to accept the situation, relieve some of the pressure, and start the process of being kind to yourself and moving forward again. The conversation will help you to appreciate that break-ups happen and that it is not your fault. It will put life into perspective and help you plan how you will approach future relationships. You will realise that not all relationships are doomed to failure; some will work, and some will not. You'll be able to learn from the experience and move on; do not dwell on it as this can only only be damaging for you and your confidence.

How to do it well: Relationship problems and breakdowns happen, and both situations can bring with them a roller coaster of emotions, some more destructive than others. But above all you must accept that the relationship is over, or that you are having problems. You may not resolve all of these problems in one day, but at least you are both talking about what is happening in your relationship and seeking ways to resolve the the problems and move forward either together or separately, if you can agree. Relationship break-ups do not heal in a day – it will take time. You can help yourself move on by talking to your best friend, your mum, dad, or an elder sibling. Tell them how you are feeling, and don't be afraid to cry or show your emotions; this is part of the recognition and healing process. The chances are it has happened to them in the past, so they will be able help you recognise that what you are feeling or the tears you are shedding are natural in the circumstances, putting the break-up into perspective.

Instead of having the conversation by phone, do it in person – go for a coffee or to the cinema. Do things that make you smile and feel good, and before long you will stop thinking about the break-up and suddenly realise that your life is back on track and you are no longer on that roller coaster of emotion. Use the experiences that you have had to make you stronger, and supportive of others who may be experiencing the same thing.

Social Networking

Social media drags us into conversations at all hours, usually when we're unprepared, and we feel a pressure to respond, engage, and disclose. The point of communication is to be understood, but written communication at a distance, from behind a screen, can lead to misunderstandings, lies, exaggerations, and bullying.

Who you should talk to: If you are having problems with social media conversations (such as unwanted attention or comments) then you might choose to talk to friends, peers, teachers, or parents. You might also have a conversation with anyone who has contact with you via social media.

What you might be feeling and thinking: The thing with social media is that there are both positive and negative aspects to its use. On the negative side, you may find yourself judging others, making fun of someone, or overreacting to posts, texts, tweets and the like. You might be saying things like, 'Did you see that post from X? What did you think?' You might just use emojis or hashtags, which completely avoid making any comment, but can be misunderstood nonetheless. You might be feeling overwhelmed with the need to keep up with other people (and their 'fascinating' lives).

When you should have this conversation: A conversation about social media use could be started by anyone, including your parents, at any time. You could also end up having the conversation with yourself when you have received an unexpected response as a reaction to something that you have posted.

Why this conversation is challenging: What is it about social media? You love using it to keep in touch with friends or to make new friends, keeping up to date with what is happening, having fun with your peers or being able to say things that you probably would not say in public! These are good things, but they can lead to reactions that you might not like or that might upset you; you may then overreact and post something that you later regret or that causes you to be 'de-friended'.

Social media can be merciless; it is easy to lose friends but very hard to regain their trust. Cyberbullying is now more commonplace; it can be difficult to deal with, leading to depression. Social media can also take over your life, to the point where your school work or your job suffers. You risk starting to judge yourself against others' appearances or lifestyles.

What will happen if you don't have the conversation: So the positive side of social media makes you smile and feel good, but what about the bullying or the pressure to be liked by your friends or peers? How is this making you feel or react? How are you dealing with it? Are you just ignoring it in the hope the negative comments will stop and the cyberbully will move on to someone else? Are you acting out of character and firing unkind comments back? In most cases, this 'antilocution' (remarks against someone made in a public setting, but not addressed directly to the target) toward you will have been building and may have started with just a mildly negative comment, but as time has gone on, the remarks have become more pointed and personal, which is now causing you some distress. You must also consider whether what you are dealing with really is a cyberbully; they may be a stalker or have more sinister intentions, and if so, doing nothing about the situation could put you in a dangerous or life-threatening position.

Whatever the case, your confidence is being affected, and you start to believe that all your friends and acquaintances on social media are laughing at you or backing the negative posts. It may have gone so far that you feel you cannot talk to anyone about it now because you will feel silly for not having done something about it before. It may have got to the stage now when you feel you can no longer face anyone for fear of receiving negative comments to your face, or of these comments spreading around the whole school, college, or work place. You may have changed your appearance drastically to fit in, perhaps stopping eating to change your body shape in an effort to please or conform. In time, you may feel that it is all too much and that maybe you should just end it all and take your own life.

What will happen if you do have the conversation: Social media overall is a great thing to be part of: it offers great contact with existing friends, can help you make new friends around the world, and helps you keep up with new trends. There are times, though, when it can backfire and become a source of distress and humiliation.

The great thing is that you can do something about the negative side of social media. Don't put up with it or try to ignore it – it will not just go away. Speak to your good friends and tell them what has happened, warning them to be careful that the same thing does not happen to them. If the harassment continues you need to make a record of the messages and the dates, so that this can be dealt with by the police. Whatever you do, speak to someone about your concerns or fears over the contact. It will not only make you less concerned, but you may also be helping others by stopping this person from preying on them.

How to do it well: There are lots of ways in which social media can be used to frighten, upset, humiliate, or torment you, but you are still in control of what you see and of the actions that you take to protect yourself. In all cases, the first thing you must do is to block that person, defriend them, or use whatever means that social media platform has to protect its users. You can in most circumstances also report the post if you feel that it is inappropriate. The best thing to do is not to respond to anything that the person misusing social media has said – just cut them off. By responding in any way, whether to rant at them or plead with them, you will only give them more ammunition to use against you. The more this happens the more frustrated, distressed, or humiliated you will get.

Make a record of the messages, posts, or texts and save it somewhere safe. If blocking them does not stop the problem, you must tell someone; this could be a trusted friend or colleague or your parents – someone who will take note and support you if needed. Whatever you do, don't just ignore the problem. Tell your trusted person how it is making you feel, and be honest: making light of the issue will not help you in the long run and may delay finding a solution or stopping the harassment from continuing.

If the police or your school / college become involved, you need to make sure that you tell them everything: the dates and content of the harassment, who you suspect or know the offender to be, how you are feeling, and whether you have responded in any way. To help with this, it's best to keep a diary and record everything, so that you remember can remember what has happened accurately and feel confident when discussing the facts with those who need to know them.

Protecting yourself from this type of cyberbullying and recognising that the other person is trying to control you in some way will give you the confidence to stand up to them and prevent them from doing it. There will be help and support all around you, and you must try not to deal with it on your own.

Pressure To Have Sex

As we mature our sexuality becomes clearer to us and our desire to find a partner increases, but just because you have reached a certain chronological age does not automatically mean that you are ready to enter a sexual relationship.

Who you should talk to: Conversations around sex and sexuality begin with yourself; you need to investigate your own feelings. Then you might have conversations with your partner. It could be that you are talking to your best friend because the question of sex has been brought up in your relationship and you do not know what to do or how you feel. You may also have a good enough relationship with your parents to be able to speak to them about how you are feeling in response to the issue – or it could be one of the most challenging conversations you may ever have to have.

What you might be feeling and thinking: Sexuality and sexual relationships are a normal and healthy part of life, but it is important to think about what you want and what you don't want, and to remain in control of your own decisions.

You may find yourself saying things like: 'I am not ready', 'No', 'Yes', 'Do you really love me?', 'You are the only one for me', 'Let's wait', 'I don't want to wait!' or 'If you don't sleep with me, then you do not love me'.

When you should have this conversation: Having this conversation may depend upon the length and depth of your relationship. If this will be your first relationship and you have no experience of sex, it is important to have the conversation about whether to make your relationship intimate at an early stage.

If you have had previous intimate relationships, it is still important to discuss at an early stage how your relationship is going to develop to avoid wrong messages and assumptions.

Why this conversation is challenging: The conversation will be probably challenging because you do not know what to do. Your emotions will be all over the place: is it the right time, is it too soon, what if we become sexually intimate and then we split up? All these thoughts and concerns may be rushing through your head. You may also be under pressure from your partner, who may be using guilt tactics on you to make you sleep with them.

On top of this, your friends may all be in sexual relationships with their partners and they may be asking you when you are going to start having sex. Peer pressure can feel very persuasive at times, but it is not necessarily right. You may have your own principles and wishes, and find it difficult to articulate them to your partner. You may have had a strict upbringing or you may for faith-based reasons be forbidden to form any sort of sexual relationship unless it's approved by your family. The fear may even extend to being ostracised – or worse, subjected to honour-based violence.

What will happen if you don't have the conversation: If you do not remain in control of your own decisions, have the choice to say 'yes' or 'no', or the time to think fully about what may happen, you may regret your actions for a long time to come. You could decide that your partner is honest and that you are the one for them and vice-versa. That's great, but have you taken the time to discuss what you'd do in case of a pregnancy? What if you are not the first partner they have slept with and they have contracted a sexually transmitted disease which they have now passed to you? Are you fully aware of the precautions to take for good sexual health? Unless you have considered all of these issues, you are opening yourself up to all sorts of consequences that can be life-changing or life-threatening.

Remaining in control means that you can decide what will happen. If you don't tell your partner when you are not comfortable about something, how will they know? Things may go further than you anticipated, which could be upsetting, humiliating, or even unlawful. No means No! If you have not had the conversation and not stayed in control of your decisions, you could find out that, thanks to your partner, everyone else in your life also knows about your intimate experiences. Gossip and social media are the best way for everyone to find out what you have been up to.

What will happen if you do have the conversation: Be honest with your partner in discussing whether to start an intimate relationship; if you don't feel that it is the right time, then say so and wait. Don't be put under pressure by either your partner or your peers. It's about what is right for you at that time. If your partner cares for you, they will respect your decision. If they make a fuss and try to use persuading tactics, then they are probably thinking more about themselves than about you. So, remain in control, and if your partner tries to coerce you and the situation doesn't feel right, then neither is that partner. It will be hard to break up, but at least you will still be in control of your life and your future.

If you both feel it is the right time, you must still discuss sexual health and the consequences of starting a sexual relationship, for example, what precautionary measures are you both going to take? Make a list of your concerns before the conversation. Decide where you will draw the line. If you feel you are not strong enough to say 'no' but that you really want to, then you must talk to someone you can trust; this could be a trusted friend, a parent, or your doctor or nurse.

How to do it well: Let's look at two conversations here – the 'yes' and the 'no'.

So you and your partner have been seeing each other for a while, you have been spending more and more time together, and you feel you would like your relationship to progress further. If it is the first time either of you is starting a sexual relationship, it will be a special moment and you should plan how you are going to bring up the question. But you should also be asking yourself whether the time is right for you both. This could depend on exams, studies, work, and a million and one other things, so think carefully to make sure that you are ready for this next step. Speak with your partner and discuss how you feel; ask them how they feel about taking the next step in the relationship. Give them time to think about it; don't expect an answer there and then. It might come as a shock or out of the blue for them, so be prepared for a reaction – although it might not be the one you expected! Don't be in a hurry to get them to answer. It is a big decision for you both to take, involving lots questions and thoughts for the future.

If you think you will be asked the question, plan your answer in advance. If it is 'yes', what do you need to discuss to keep you both safe and in good sexual health? What about contraception or other precautionary measures? Bear in mind that some religions and cultures do not allow its use. More importantly, are you ready to start a family, as there is a 30% chance of pregnancy from one-off sexual intercourse?

Make sure it is something that you both want. If your answer is 'no', you will need to plan how you are going to say this without causing yourself or your partner too much distress. Be honest, explain why now is not the right time and be prepared for the possibility of an overreaction, but you must remain in control of how the relationship progresses; don't be bullied or coerced into changing your mind and having sex if you don't want to. If your partner insists without your consent, threatens or uses violence against you, then for your own safety you need to leave and go to friends or somewhere you feel safe, or contact the emergency services immediately.

There is also the possibility that your partner will take the decision to end the relationship because you have said 'no'. They may threaten and insult you because they are not in control of you; you must stay calm and in control of your emotions and decisions. Again, do not give in to their behaviour; find a safe way to leave the situation and go somewhere that you feel safe.

Body Image Issues

Body image is someone's idea of what they look like. It's like a photo that you have in your mind of what you think other people see when they look at you. Sometimes this image is distorted. Body image issues affect people of all genders.

Who you should talk to: You may not be talking to anyone but yourself, although you are more than likely listening to everyone else and taking all their comments and hurtfulness to heart. You might want to talk to your parents and close friends.

What you might be feeling and thinking: Have you heard yourself or a friend saying things like, 'I'm too tall', 'I'm too short', 'I'm too skinny', 'I'm too fat', or 'No one likes me because I am too fat or too thin'? Teenagers tend to be particularly conscious of the way they look, and their body image can be linked to how they feel about themselves as a person. They may feel that they cannot join their friends in groups because of their size. They may feel embarrassed and insecure over the way they look and then start to obsess about their body image. They may worry constantly about being laughed at, and this can prevent them from doing what they want to do.

Society and the media also have a big part to play in the problem of body image, as there is still a lot of pressure to look a certain way, to be skinnier, to be able to wear certain clothes and to have a current hairstyle or tattoo.

When you should have this conversation: The conversation can take place at any time. You may see a photo of a model or celebrity and think, 'I wish I could look like that and be able to wear that type of outfit.' Someone in your family may make a passing comment about looks or size and you might find yourself distressed even though it was not aimed at you. Your friends could just be joking with you about your appearance and you could be joining in, but in reality you might be very unhappy. If you are the target of bullies, you will need to have the conversation with a trusted friend, teacher, elder sibling, or parent.

Why this conversation is challenging: The shape and size of a person's body are linked to many things and there is little you can do about that. At puberty your shape can change almost overnight, your hormones start playing up, and it can be pretty difficult just to deal with those changes. Different ethnic backgrounds can have predispositions for different body shapes in both men and women, and there is little you can do about that either. The challenge is accepting that your body is your own, and it can and will change shape throughout your life. Try to focus on being healthy and positive about your body and mind, and rather than on what others say.

Young people are fearful of others' opinions of them as they want desperately to fit in and be part of a group, to be liked and to be respected. This is not always easy if they have a negative view of themselves because of poor self-esteem, pressure from friends and family, school life, and, of course, social media and media images in general.

What will happen if you don't have the conversation: Body image is linked to self-esteem, which can be easily destroyed or diminished by the actions of others. The more you are told that you have a problem with your appearance, the more you will believe it and the more your self-esteem will suffer. You may become depressed and isolated, and start to lose friends as you shut yourself away. You may find yourself overreacting to the pressures and developing health-related problems like bulimia, anorexia, or comfort eating. You may seek out surgery to change the shape of your body or your facial appearance, which will cost money, and becoming addicted to surgery could lead you into financial difficulty, with the risk of losing everything to pay off the debts that you have accrued.

What will happen if you do have the conversation: You need to discuss your worries, as you will mostly not be able to change the aspect of your body that is distressing you. You may be able to adjust your lifestyle to make you fitter and healthier, but the most important thing to do is to improve your self-esteem and start to feel good about yourself. When you've identified what or who is causing the dent in your self-esteem, you can start to rebuild it, recognising that you are what matters and what others think does not matter. If they are concerned about your health, though, involve them in helping you to improve it.

Having high self-esteem will mean that you feel good about yourself, it will promote good mental health, and it will teach you much more about yourself and your likes and dislikes. You will be able to be realistic about your body, and find friends who like and respect you for who you are. You will be in control of your life and destiny.

How to do it well: You need to start by identifying what it is that is making you feel bad about yourself.

By this I don't mean your perception of your body image. What I mean who or what is making you feel bad and destroying your self-esteem. Is it school, work, bullies, family or friends, social media, or another source?

Once you have pinpointed the cause you will need to speak to someone you trust to start getting your confidence back and rebuilding your self-esteem. You may find that someone completely new could be the best person to guide and encourage you. Sometimes it is those closest to us who cause us the most pain, not because they intend to but because they think they are being helpful.

You will already have identified the things that are making you feel bad; you must now must express these to your trusted person. It may help to have a written list to share with them. Tell them how you are feeling and the effect this is having on you. Listen to what they say, but remember it is you who are in control. Find out what makes you happy and remember these things every each time you begin having negative thoughts about yourself, to prevent yourself from being unhappy.

Talk to yourself about your body, giving yourself constructive comments and upbeat suggestions. You need to build your positive body image by thinking about encouraging and supportive comments. To help with this, give yourself at least three compliments every day, focusing on the good things that you have done that day. Talk positively about yourself to others and be confident – after all, it is *your* body. This will also help to change the way you view yourself. Focus on all the positive aspects of your body and what it can do; *don't* focus on all the things that you think are wrong with it or the things that you want to change.

By being confident about your body, you will learn to love yourself. Humans are diverse and come in all shapes, sizes, makes, and models, just like everything else in nature. *None of us is perfect, and you need to remember that.* If you must still change something about your body, make a list of the things that you can genuinely change and the things that you can't. Set yourself realistic goals to work toward achieving the changes that are possible. If you struggle with sticking to your goals, then share them with your trusted friends and family to help keep you on track. You must not fall into the trap of thinking that this will happen overnight, but by starting to love yourself and not trying to be someone else you will build your confidence and self-esteem and see the beautiful person that you really are.

Summary

There are hundreds of conversations to be had, around hundreds of different issues. You'll see from the conversation examples above that many of the most challenging conversations begin in our heads, where we hold conversations with ourselves. Learning to talk to yourself in a positive way is one of the most important life skills. Then use the SPEAK method to think about where, how, and when to have the right conversation, with the right person, being respectful of their feelings and ensuring yours are respected too. These conversation skills need to be practised; you'll learn with each conversation, and your skills will grow. Be confident about having conversations.

Conclusions

'Understanding comes through communication, and through understanding we find the way to peace.'
— **Ralph C. Smedley**

Where do you go from here?

You have taken the first step to find out more about conversations, why they can fail, and how you can better prepare for your next conversation. The next step is to practise those new-found skills and experiment with what works for you. It may be that starting a conversation is not a problem for you, as you are friendly and approachable, but sustaining a conversation by asking open questions and listening might be your area for development; if so, concentrate on practising this.

Don't be afraid to ask your friends and family for feedback on your asking of open questions; this will be the only way for you to find out that you are not actually asking open questions but are closing conversations down. Practise listening to news programmes: can you repeat what has been said or, as the saying goes, did it just go in one ear and out the other? This will not only increase your knowledge, it will also improve your listening skills. If it is the television news, watch out for those NVCs: Is the reporter or the person they are talking to comfortable and confident about their story? Is their body language conveying the same message as their words?

Have a go at mind mapping or using the sticky notes to explore your thoughts – or you may find a better way. Start with something easy or straightforward to get the hang of it; for example, what goals are you going to set yourself for the short, medium and long term? Where do you see yourself next year or in five years' time, and how are you going to achieve this? Don't put if off or you will never do it; you will find an excuse to do something else.

Your CV, applications, and résumé, for example, will also need some planning, and you will probably end up getting frustrated with the first few drafts and deleting them. Again, start with the easy things and build on this once you have a solid foundation. This solid foundation could be the basis for all the other details that you change, depending on the application or CV you are preparing.

Above all, keep those conversations flowing: the challenging ones, the ones with those you love, the ones that reach out to new people, the ones with people who can help you, and the conversations that you can offer to help other people.

Conversations are what make us human.

Share Your Success

I hope that you have enjoyed the journey I have taken you on and that it has given you the tools to improve your conversation skills and general observation skills during conversations.

If you have enjoyed this book or have any feedback or suggestions, or if you would like further information, please do not hesitate to contact me at:

info@speakwithinfluence.co.uk

I would also love to hear of your successes based on the advice in this book. Please feel free to send me your stories about how the tips worked for you.

If you do get in touch, I may contact you (with your permission) to find out more and might want to feature your story on the *Speak with Influence* website or any future publication, so please include your details.

If you are at school or college and feel that this information would help others, then please share the knowledge you have learned. If I can help in any way, then please contact me to let me know.

If you are a teacher or lecturer and you feel it would be useful to your students if I ran a masterclass at your venue, then please contact me for details and to discuss your needs.

Resources

All the fact sheets, tasks and exercises can be found on my website. You can download them for free at: https://www.speakwithinfluence.co.uk/learning-support/

There are so many different organisations and helpful sites that are available for anyone to use for help and support, and I have listed a few below. Some will go into great detail, and others will keep the information straightforward. Depending on how much you want to learn, you can also use different words in the search engines and see what comes up.

Sources Of Support

Counselling and crisis support

www.anti-bullyingalliance.org.uk

www.bullying.co.uk

www.lifelinehelpline.info

www.samaritans.org

www.papyrus-uk.org

www.themix.org.uk

Education

www.thestudentroom.co.uk

www.ucl.ac.uk

Family

www.childline.org

www.eachaction.org.uk

www.familylives.org.uk

www.nspcc.org.uk

Health

www.beateatingdisorders.org.uk

www.healthtalk.org

www.nhs.uk/conditions

www.nice.org.uk/guidance

www.teenweightwise.com

www.weightconcern.com

www.youngpeopleshealth.org.uk

Mental health

www.metanoia.org

www.mindingyourhead.info

www.theblackdog.net

www.thecalmzone.net

www.youngminds.org.uk

Relationships

www.relate.org.uk

Skills and employment

www.acas.org.uk

www.bbc.co.uk/skillswise/english

www.improveyoursocialskills.com

www.monster.co.uk

https://nationalcareersservice.direct.gov.uk

www.reed.co.uk

www.skillsyouneed.com

Miscellaneous

www.premier.org.uk

www.ted.com/talks

www.wikihow

Bibliography and Further Reading

Printed Resources

Adler, R, Rosenfeld, L, and Proctor, R (2001). *Interplay: The Process of Interpersonal Communicating,* 8th edn, Fort Worth, Texas: Harcourt.

Carver, RP, Johnson, RI, and Friedman HL (1971). 'Factor Analysis of the Ability to Comprehend Time-compressed Speech', *Journal of Reading Behaviour,* 4/1, 40–49.

Fisher, RP, and Geisel man, RE (1992). *Memory-enhancing Techniques for Investigative Interviewing: The Cognitive Interview,* Springfield, Illinois, Charles C Thomas.

Houseman, RC, Galvin, M and Prescott, D (1988). *Business Communication: Strategies and Skills*, Chicago, Holt, Rinehart & Winston.

Mehrabian, A (1981). *Silent Messages: Implicit Communication of Emotions and Attitudes*, Belmont, California, Wadsworth.

Parker, M (2014). *It's Not What You Say, It's The Way You Say It!* London, Vermillion.

Pellegrino, F, Coupe, C and Marico, E (2011). 'Across-language Perspective on Speech Information Rate', *Language*, 87/3, 539–558.

Shepherd, E (2007). *Investigative Interviewing: The Conversation Management Approach*, Oxford, Oxford University Press.

Online resources

www.acs-schools.com/university-admissions-officers-report-2017

www.gla.ac.uk/news/archiveofnews/2014/february/headline_306019_en.html

www.theglasshammer.com/2017/01/31/takes-seven-seconds-make-good-first-impression

www.kent.ac.uk/ces/advice.html

www.4h.okstate.edu / literature-links / lit-online / others

www.ofcom.org.uk / research-and-data / multi-sector-research / cmr / cmr-2018 / report

www.ofcom.org.uk / research-and-data / multi-sector-research / general-communications / consumer-engagement-with-communication-services

www.princeton.edu / news / 2006 / 08 / 22 / snap-judgments-decide-faces-character-psychologist-finds

www.scribd.com / document / 344335262 / Albert-Mehrabian-s-communications-model

www.simplemind.eu

www.thenextgreatgeneration.com /: The Way We Communicate: Pros and Cons: Shauna Stacy (2011)

www.tonybuzan.com / ?s=mind+mapping

MIND MAPS is registered to the Buzan Organization under 'Organising and conducting courses in personal and intellectual awareness and methods of self-improvement', all included in Class 41 UK00001424476 (1993).

www.trainingfolks.com / blog / bid / 307362 / Training-Consultants-Effective-Communication-Part-2

Acknowledgements

My thanks to:

My partner and driving force, Maria, who gave me belief in my abilities.

My family, especially my nephews and their partners, for their feedback on the first draft.

Mike Dance, a good friend, who was honest about the content.

Shaa Wasmund and Kym Vincenti, for giving me the push to Get It Done!

Lucy, Joe and everyone at Rethink Press who have made this book the best it can be through their help, support and guidance.

Special thanks to Janine Antoine, Dr Nicole Howse and Dr Sam Parsons for their help, support and feedback on the conversation cases.

The Author

Helen Ponting is a for-
mer police supervisor
and served for many
years in the Royal Air
Force. She is also a
qualified trainer, asses-
sor, and an Internal
Quality Assessor with a
BA (Hons) in Education
and a Postgraduate
Certificate in Education.

Helen's knowledge and experience are diverse;
she has a passion for helping people to reach their
potential, with a focus on leadership skills and personal development. Her career as an operational

police officer and trainer has allowed her to develop her skills and knowledge in communication and in managing and planning people's interactions; her coaching and development skills have helped a wide variety of people at different stages of their careers.

Helen aims to share this knowledge and help young people to develop and achieve their goals, or simply improve their skills, by giving them a toolkit to use in a wide variety of situations or interactions with others.

Get in touch with Helen if you need help developing or changing your communication style. You can contact her with your questions at:

www.speakwithinfluence.co.uk

info@speakwithinfluence.co.uk

www.facebook.com/speakwithinfluence/

40516982R00114

Printed in Poland
by Amazon Fulfillment
Poland Sp. z o.o., Wrocław